MY
PRAYER
CHAIR

A LIVING, WALKING, BREATHING RELATIONSHIP WITH JESUS

D1600593

My Prayer Chair
— A Living, Walking, Breathing Relationship with Jesus
Copyright ©2014 by Carla McDougal
2nd Edition

Published by RLMPublishing, a division of Reflective Life
Ministries 6606 FM 1488 Ste 148-185 Magnolia, TX 77354

Hebrew/Greek definitions are from Strong's Concordance of the
Bible.

ISBN: 978-1-63296-023-8

Printed in the United States

To contact Carla McDougal go to:

www.reflectivelifeministries.org

DEDICATION & ACKNOWLEDGMENTS

My Prayer Chair is dedicated to Ada Belle Yeargan-Wills, my Grandmama. Her love and devotion to prayer left a mark on all her children and grandchildren. She entered the world in 1906 and went to be with her Lord and Savior, Jesus, in 1991. Her eighty-five years filled all of us with joy, wisdom, and strength.

I love you, Grandmama!

Carla McDougal

A huge love-hug goes to my husband, Fred. "Your love, encouragement, and prayers spur me forward in accomplishing God's call on my life."

I send kisses and blessings to my children. "I thank God for all of you. I thank Him for answering my heart's cry for you to love Jesus with all your hearts, souls, minds, and strength."

My heart of appreciation goes out to Kitty Self for fine-tuning *My Prayer Chair*. "Thank you for helping me to express my creative ideas more clearly."

A big "Thank You" to Jake Allen for developing the *My Prayer Chair* book-cover design.

Love working with both of you so much!

CONTENTS

*Looking to use *My Prayer Chair* as a

Bible study for a small group?

Download the free *My Prayer Chair Leader's*

Guide (PDF) at <u>www.reflectivelifeministries.org</u>

The Heart of
My Prayer Chair

Only be careful, and watch yourselves closely so that you do not forget the things your eyes have seen or let them slip from your heart as long as you live. Teach them to your children and to their children after them.

– Deuteronomy 4:9

Childhood memories. Teachable moments. Overflowing love. Images of the old black, wooden rocker linger in the depths of my mind. Blemishes and discoloration marked years of teetering to and fro. As early as I can remember, this chair played an important role in my life. Not the chair itself, but what it represented. In my grandmama's words, "This is my prayer chair." To be totally honest, I didn't understand the significance of its name until years later... in God's perfect timing.

In my younger days, climbing into Grandmama's lap created a place of comfort, a refuge like no other. Without saying a word, I would bury my head into her chest as she rocked back and forth, gently whistling the tender hymn *In the Garden*. A sweet sanctuary of unconditional love.

Time seemed to move so fast. Through high school, college, and then marriage, visits to Grandmama's house lessened. Blessings flowed more frequently through our phone conversations. One call in particular resonates in my soul. While rocking my firstborn child, memories of Grandmama poured over me. Warmth consumed my heart, so I immediately called her. After our sweet hellos, I asked about her day. To my surprise, her familiar answer penetrated like never before... "I'm in my prayer chair."

Like a light illuminating its surroundings, her words ignited a flame of understanding. All my life she referred to her old rocker as her prayer chair, but I never really grasped her meaning until that moment. Right then, the vision of her teetering back and forth, as she laid her requests before her Lord, left an imprint on my heart forever. I've since wondered how many miles her prayer chair accumulated over the years.

On this memorable day, my grandmama passed a torch to the next generation... a torch fueled by prayer. Tears blur my vision as I recall her loving and powerful impact on my life. Today I have a prayer chair of my own. It doesn't look anything like

Grandmama's, but it provides the same purpose. Numerous praises, prayer requests, and intercessions take place while I'm snuggled in my prayer chair. Most of my articles, blogs, books, and devotionals are composed while nestled in its comfort. In fact, all the entries in this book were written while I rested in this sweet haven. Oh, the heart of *My Prayer Chair* represents major stepping-stones in my walk with Jesus.

This book, *My Prayer Chair,* encourages the reader to engage in an ongoing conversation with God seven days a week, twenty-four hours a day. Jesus bridges the pathway of communication between His Father and believers. The minute we receive Jesus into our lives, the Holy Spirit is indwelled in us forever. The Spirit breathes life into our relationships with Jesus. He serves as our counselor, guide, and teacher, continuously pointing us to the King of kings and Lord of lords, Jesus. Prayer activates our relationships with God through Jesus, inspired by the Holy Spirit. God gives His children the opportunity to participate in eternity here on earth through prayer.

PRAYER CHALLENGE

Read Romans 8:26,27 and John 14:15-17 and 16:5-15. Before reading, ask the Holy Spirit to give you insight into God's Word. Make this a habit, to pray before you ever open your Bible. The Spirit reveals the mysteries of God. Add this same process to reading each entry of this little book. May the Lord bless your journey through *My Prayer Chair.*

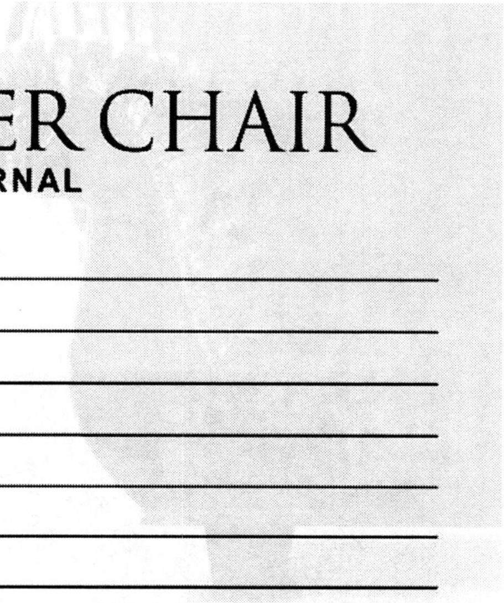

MY PRAYER CHAIR

JOURNAL

_____

_____

_____

_____

_____

_____

_____

_____

_____

_____

_____

_____

_____

_____

_____

_____

_____

_____

_____

WHY PRAY?

Show me your ways, O Lord, teach me your paths; guide me in your truth and teach me, for you are God my Savior, and my hope is in you all day long.

— Psalm 25:4-5

The power of prayer. Really? Does prayer have power? If so, how? Why do we pray if God knows all the answers? Why do we communicate with Him if He is in control of everything in heaven and on earth? Why do we pray in Jesus' name?

My Prayer Chair focuses on God's call for an intimate relationship with His children. Believers in Jesus need to breathe, walk, and live in constant communication with the One who gives us eternal life. Frequent conversations with Him focus our hearts, minds, and souls on Him.

Meditate on this quote from Jennifer Kennedy Dean, "Prayer releases the will of God bringing His will out of the spiritual realm and causing it to take effect in the material realm. Prayer opens the way for God to do what He longs to do. When God wants to change the course events will take on their own, He calls out an intercessor."[1]

In many cases, God waits for us to pray, praise His Holy name, stand in the gap, call out to Him, listen to the groaning of the Holy Spirit, and intercede for others. He is actively working to bring His will to fruition. As a result, after we lay our requests at His feet, we trust He is actively at work bringing His will into motion. Ephesians 3:20-21 provides a powerful message to God's children, *Now to Him who is able to do immeasurably more than all we ask or imagine, according to His power that is at work within us, to Him be the glory in the church and in Christ Jesus throughout all generations, for ever and ever! Amen.*

In my Bible study, *Reflecting Him: Living for Jesus and Loving It*, I share how prayer changed my life. Please read this excerpt from Week 1, Reflections In Life: Images in the Mirror...

> *God, help! What is wrong with me? Why do I feel this way?* On the outside everything appeared in order—spiritual life, marriage, children, friends, health. Yet inside, the feeling of death simmered... not a physical death, but a living death. My joy slowly faded into the darkness. *But I am a Christian. I love Jesus. How can I have these thoughts?* No one knew. I put on a facemask as part of my daily attire. That superficial smile looked very real on this thirty-three-year-old woman!
>
> *Can't he see what he is doing to me? He needs to be more sensitive!* My marriage teetered back and forth. Laughter withered away. To my way of thinking, our problems existed because

---

[1] Jennifer Kennedy Dean. *Live a Praying Life.* (New Hope Publishers, 2004), 25-26.

of my husband. I thought we needed marriage counseling.

It is two a.m. These clothes must be folded. The dishes need washing. Look at these toys all over the floor. I can't go to sleep until everything is done! I can't halt my life! I must keep going. Mothering four young children required love, discipline, and steadfastness. I knew they needed me. I turned off the light and curled up in the corner of the playroom. Tears poured. God, help! This is all I prayed and all God wanted — my surrendered heart.

Depression? Are you sure? I don't even take naps during the day. In fact, I hardly sleep at all. Christians don't have depression problems. Joy is part of our job description! Yes, I believed the lie that Christians couldn't be depressed. Are you ready for this? I believed a Christian who struggled with depression just needed a stronger relationship with Jesus. There wasn't a book or a lecture that could change my opinion. Little did I know, God needed to teach me a thing or two about humility and compassion! So in His tender way, He allowed me to experience firsthand this dreaded thing called depression. He walked me through each step, teaching me to trust Him. In time, I realized I couldn't blame anyone for my condition — not my family, not God. The Lord used the doctors and medicines to bring physical healing. In turn, this healing allowed me to grow deeper in my walk with the Lord. As a result, I come before you a humbled woman. I thank God for bringing me through my depression. Knowing where I used to be in my life and where I am today brings tears to my eyes. As I reflect on this experience, I realize God embedded His promise in my heart. Deuteronomy 31:6 states, *He will never leave you nor forsake you.* Amen.

With a shout of joy I can say God rescued me from the pit of depression when I was thirty-five. I asked the Lord to use my past for His glory. I desired to be a light in the darkness for others experiencing this same hopelessness. I prayed for the Holy Spirit to reveal to me those who needed prayer. I found the more I prayed, the more I reflected Jesus. I craved to know

Him, read His word, praise His name, and worship Him!

Never in a million years did I think God would use me to serve Him. No way, not me! I mean, look at my past. However, about five years after my battle with depression, I experienced a stirring within my heart. In my quiet times with God, I sensed Him telling me to share my story—not with one woman, but groups of women. For about a year I didn't share this with anyone, not even my husband. Why? Fear gripped me. Over and over I talked with God about this pull on my heart. I shared my weaknesses with Him, as if He didn't know them already. I heard Him whisper, "When you are weak, I am strong." Then I reminded Him of my past experiences. He answered, "All for My glory." Finally, I knew this next question would change His mind: "God, what about my dyslexia? I can't read the Bible in front of people." His response, "I know. I will do it for you, just as I helped Moses speak to crowds of people." In that moment I realized when God says, "Surrender it all!" He means everything. And we need to expect the unexpected.

With my body trembling, I finally shared all these thoughts and prayers with my man. I honestly believed he would advise me against moving forward. But to my surprise, he supported God's call for me to minister to women. Still doubting, however, I pleaded with God to give me an outward sign. You know, like a burning bush! A couple of weeks later I mentioned my need for prayer to some of my girlfriends. Before I could explain why, one of them said she knew the request. These words flowed from her lips, "Carla, God is calling you to be a Christian women's speaker!" I almost fell out of my chair as I said, "How did you know?" My sweet friend next to her said, "For the past five years, I prayed God would call you into this ministry." The Holy Spirit's sweet and tender presence immediately penetrated each of our souls. A shared memory—the power of God—a moment to behold! At that point, in the quiet of my heart, I realized God has a plan for each of us. He writes the pages of our life stories, all for His glory. All He asks is for us to give

Him access to do His will. Doubt flooded my mind as fear emerged. Again, these same words flowed from my mouth: "God, help!" This is all I prayed and all God wanted—my surrendered heart.

God, you have to be joking! Write a Bible study? Not me! Again, I resisted God's call. I shared with Him why, in my opinion, He needed a different vessel for this project. I am not a writer. You must mean someone else. Remember my reading disability? I started debating with God again. Then one day I read a verse that opened the curtain to a play in my heart. Before me on stage, God sang these words through 2 Corinthians 3:18, *And we, who with unveiled faces all reflect the Lord's glory, are being transformed into his likeness with ever-increasing glory, which comes from the Lord, who is the Spirit.* Applauding, I shouted, "God, help!" This is all I prayed and all God wanted—my surrendered heart.

With hands lifted high and shouts of praise in my heart, I am committed to reflecting Him! I desire to live my life sold out to Jesus. It humbles me to think of all He has done, is doing, and will do. He rescued me from the pit of despair and saved me from the trenches of darkness. Jesus is the Way, the Truth, and the Life! I am so excited about Living for Jesus and Loving It![2]

PRAYER CHALLENGE

Open your heart to all the Holy Spirit wants to teach you through *My Prayer Chair*. Ask the Lord to give you a heart of understanding and a desire to seek Him fully. Watch for ways to grow in your walk with Jesus. Never forget to thank Him along the way.

Listening for God, while you are praying, opens the door for Him to accomplish His purposes in your life—all for His glory.

---

[2] McDougal, Carla. Reflecting Him: Living for Jesus and Loving It! (RLMPublishing) 1-3.

MY PRAYER CHAIR
JOURNAL

_____
_____
_____
_____
_____
_____
_____
_____
_____
_____
_____
_____
_____
_____
_____
_____
_____
_____
_____
_____
_____

PRAYER CONSULTANT

In the same way, the Spirit helps us in our weakness. We do not know what we ought to pray for, but the Spirit Himself intercedes for us through wordless groans. And He who searches our hearts knows the mind of the Spirit, because the Spirit intercedes for God's people in accordance with the will of God.
— Romans 8:26-27

How do we know what to pray? How does prayer work? Let's look at it this way—a believer's Prayer Consultant is the Holy Spirit. God gives His children the Holy Spirit to connect us to a

16

deeper, more intimate relationship with Himself through Jesus. The Holy Spirit is likened to the blood veins in our bodies. Just as the veins carry the blood through the human body, so the Holy Spirit is the conduit for our relationships with Jesus. He teaches us how and what to pray. The more we listen to the Holy Spirit, the more our prayer lives become God focused instead of me focused.

Remember, we receive the Holy Spirit the minute we accept Jesus into our lives. He is there always and forever. He serves as our counselor, guide, and teacher, continuously pointing us to the King of kings and Lord of lords, Jesus. Prayer activates our relationships with God through Jesus, inspired by the Holy Spirit.

With this in mind, read my example of how the Holy Spirit directed me to pray, and what he taught me through this powerful experience. *Reflecting Him,* Week 5, Prayer from the Inside Out, Day 4: The Living Room—

> I cannot go another day without sharing a special moment between the Lord and me. While writing Day 1 of Prayer from the Inside Out, I prayed, "Lord, I don't know how I am going to afford to get this Bible study published. Lack of funds is a big problem, but I trust You to handle this dilemma. If You provide the funds, I am going to praise You, and if the study doesn't get published, I am going to praise You. No matter what the outcome, our time together working on this project has been wonderful! Amen!"
>
> Two days later, I received a phone call. A dear friend of more than twenty years said her husband wanted to visit with me. In our conversation, he shared how his corporation was dedicated to furthering God's kingdom. His management

team prays to find ministries with the same vision. Then he continued, "After taking a look at the heart of Reflective Life Ministries, we would like to support your ministry in the amount of _____."

His actions followed Ephesians 3:20-21, ...*to him who is able to do immeasurably more than all we ask or imagine.* I was speechless! All I could think about was my prayer forty-eight hours prior to this conversation, and how I said, "Lord, this Bible study is Yours. I trust You to do what You want with it."

He then said to me, "How big do you think God is, Carla? Open the door and let God go beyond what your mind can conceive. Continue to do all He is calling you to do for His kingdom. Encourage women to live their lives sold out to Jesus. Use your God-given talents for His glory!"

I cried for two days! It was not because of the amount of money. It was God's provision. God used this on-the-spot training to teach me to pray and then let go so God could do His work. I pray this encourages you as you pray for situations in your life. Don't miss a moment when the Holy Spirit is prompting you to pray. He has some on-the-spot training for you as well![3]

---

[3] McDougal, Carla. Reflecting Him: Living for Jesus and Loving It! (RLMPublishing) 105.

PRAYER CHALLENGE

Before you begin praying, ask the Holy Spirit to reveal how to pray, what to pray, and who needs prayer. Blessings flow through this process. Over time this becomes a habit. As a result, your prayer life changes to a twenty-four hours a day, seven days a week living, walking, breathing relationship with Jesus. Begin now drawing nearer to Him in prayer.

No eye has seen, no ear has heard, no mind has conceived what God has prepared for those who love him, but God has revealed it to us by his Spirit. The Spirit searches all things, even the deep things of God. For who among men knows the thoughts of a man except the man's spirit within him? In the same way no one knows the thoughts of God except the Spirit of God.

—1 Cor. 2:9-11

MY PRAYER CHAIR
JOURNAL

_____

_____

_____

_____

_____

_____

_____

_____

_____

_____

_____

_____

_____

_____

_____

_____

_____

_____

_____

GENERATION TO GENERATION

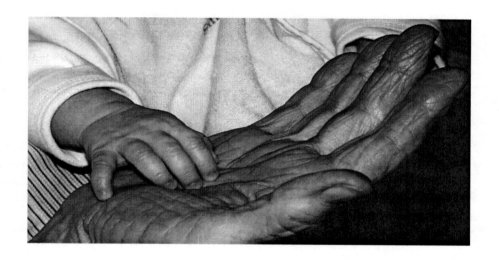

One generation shall praise Your works to another, and shall declare Your mighty acts.

— Psalm 145:4 (NKJV)

Have you experienced a family reunion—the kind that represents all branches of your family tree? A gathering where one generation passes down the family stories and history to the next generation?

I love big family reunions! Every summer my dad's family holds the Lucas Family Reunion. For over fifty years this gathering repeatedly attracts at least one hundred relatives. My great-great grandfather was one of eighteen siblings, seventeen boys and one girl. Can you imagine the enormous meals their mama prepared every day? What about the piles of laundry using only a scrub board and washtub? I get tired just thinking about it.

A few years ago at one of our reunions, God opened my eyes to a vital truth. After a conversation with my great-great uncle, ninety-five years old, I realized my family lineage is packed with believers in Jesus Christ. His tender stories of the past confirmed my Christian heritage. At one point his eyes welled-up as he shared about the family Bible and the family's prayer times together.

All of a sudden, Psalm 145:4 popped into my mind, *One generation shall praise Your works to another, and shall declare Your mighty acts.* In that moment, I realized I am a product of the generations before me. Chill bumps, or I refer to them as God bumps, encompassed my whole body. Thoughts poured in like, "What prayers did my ancestors pray years ago that God is answering today? Did my great-great-great grandmother ask the Lord to capture the hearts of the children of her offspring for generations to come? Are these prayers still coming to fruition?" Words can't describe this moment of revelation. Inwardly, I thanked the Lord for this family and His heart of love.

Almost immediately, conviction overwhelmed me. God impressed on me the importance of imparting this same truth to my children, and their children, and so on. Prayer is a key component in passing the message of Jesus to the following generations. I cried out to God on behalf of my children, for each one to marry the one God chooses, so as husband and wife, they can pass on the love of Jesus to their children. A prayer ignited for my grandchildren to be mighty men and women for the Kingdom of God.

Then this thought burst into my mind, "After I am in heaven with Jesus, the only way I can still affect the generations that follow is through the prayers I prayed while living on this earth!" Tears emerge. Heart warms. God bumps ignite. We see this over and over in God's Word where God's promise is fulfilled in the generations to follow. For example, Jesus prayed in John 17 for future believers in Him, which includes believers today. Wow, His prayer is still coming to fruition.

PRAYER CHALLENGE

Pray for your family members to love the Lord with all their hearts, all their minds, and all their strength. Pray that this love for Jesus passes on to their children and their children. Ask the Lord how to pray for your family heritage. You just might be the Prayer Warrior the Lord uses to redirect the focus of the next generation!

MY PRAYER CHAIR
JOURNAL

_____

_____

_____

_____

_____

_____

_____

_____

_____

_____

_____

_____

_____

_____

_____

_____

_____

_____

_____

MY PRAYER CLOSET

As for me, far be it from me that I should sin against the Lord by failing to pray for you. And I will teach you the way that is good and right. But be sure to fear the Lord and serve Him faithfully with all your heart; consider what great things He has done for you.

—1 Samuel 12:23-24

A brief encounter lasting only a moment, but never forgotten. A lump forms in my throat. Humbleness envelops my heart. Let me set the scene.

It's Saturday morning. Errands filled my agenda. Pulling out of the driveway, I prayed, "Lord, I don't want to miss a moment with

You." This prayer continued marinating in my heart as I blurted out, "What do you have planned? I can't wait to find out!"

Within minutes I approached a busy intersection. Noticing the light turning yellow, I slowed down. All of a sudden, out of nowhere, two ladies wearing bright yellow shirts darted out in front of my car. I slammed on my brakes. Taking a deep breath, I noticed the first woman running to the car beside me while the other woman approached my door. I hesitated for a split second, but rolled down the window. I must admit I was a little apprehensive.

Then it happened. A quickening in my spirit sparked a moment of tenderness. In this brief encounter, the young woman shared her testimony...

> "Hi! My name is Crystal. Jesus saved me from the pit of drug addiction. I represent this powerful Houston ministry—a faith based Christian organization that reaches out to those suffering from drug and alcohol addiction. A place addicts can be rehabilitated through the power of Jesus."

Our conversation continued, "So Crystal, are you a believer?" I asked. Her face radiated as she replied, "Yes Ma'am, my Jesus set me free! He's my Lord and Savior." Tears welled up in both of us. Without realizing it, I grabbed her hands and pulled her head into the car window. An outpouring of prayer gushed from my lips, "Thank You, Jesus, for saving Crystal. I praise you for rescuing her from drugs. I ask for Your protection over her and that the enemy never get a foothold again in her life. And... " By now, Crystal was praying too. Right then I realized God answered my prayer with this brief encounter at a red light.

Don't forget, all of this happened between a red light and a green light, in less than three minutes. Hmm, I can't help but wonder if God tweaked the timing of that light for a special divine appointment. The light turned green, we hugged, and I proceeded

26

through the intersection. Oh, and of course I donated to the ministry with a heart full of love.

Glancing into the rear-view mirror, I observed a sight I will never forget. Crystal jumped into the air with her arms reaching to the sky as if to say, "Praise you, Lord Jesus. Thank you for loving me enough to allow a special brief encounter with a sister-in-Christ!" Needless to say, a smile adorned my face, warmth embraced my soul, and praises filled the car.

Immediately thoughts rolled in, "Did anyone else notice this meeting? If so, what were they thinking?" Tears gently fell. I was overwhelmed, humbled, and amazed at how quickly God answered my morning prayer. My car serves a multitude of purposes... even as my prayer closet!

PRAYER CHALLENGE

Do you use your car as a prayer closet? Try praying while you drive. Use this time to commune with the Lord. "Lord, I don't want to miss a moment with You. What do you have planned? I can't wait to find out!" Be ready. Be willing. Be watchful!

MY PRAYER CHAIR

JOURNAL

_____

_____

_____

_____

_____

_____

_____

_____

_____

_____

_____

_____

_____

_____

_____

_____

_____

_____

_____

_____

IN THE SILENCE

Lord, I wait for you; You will answer, Lord My God.
— Psalm 38:15

Silence. Why is this so difficult?

Can you remember a time you prayed with all your heart about something? Possibly you prayed for years and years. Maybe it seemed as if your prayers just hit the ceiling and bounced back. In all honesty, this can be discouraging! In fact, at this point many give up and throw in the towel.

Silence. How do we trust when we don't see results?

Corrie Ten Boom was a Nazi prison camp survivor who watched her sister suffer and die during their imprisonment. She barely survived herself. Despite all her trials, she forgave her abusers and continued to trust in God. Her life story is a picture of living, walking, and breathing Jesus. Through difficult and life threatening situations, her faith in God never wavered. She trusted Him even when she didn't see immediate results. How? She believed in who God was, not in what He could do for her. She trusted God's Word twenty-four hours a day, seven days a week. Her faith wasn't based on what God was doing in her life, but in the character of God. Even in desperate circumstances, her walk with Jesus remained strong. She focused on Him, not the situation. As a result, her life example continues to encourage others, many years after her death.

Silence. Sometimes in the stillness, God is doing His greatest work.

I understand the silence of depression. The haunting memories linger close to my heart and mind. In this season it seemed difficult for me to hear from God. Deeper and deeper I spiraled into this pit. I prayed, but no answers. I asked, but no response. My thoughts escalated out of control until one day I screamed, "God, Help!" And He showed up in a mighty way. Little did I know He allowed this time of what I call "silence" to be one of the greatest teachable times in my life.

God calls us to listen to Him. Trust His plan. Surrender it all, with no strings attached. Cast your cares upon Him.

In the silence…

> *Pray*. Continue to lift your requests before Him.

> *Trust*. God is in the midst of accomplishing His purposes for His glory.

> *Praise*. Praise Him before the answer is revealed.

PRAYER CHALLENGE

Do you feel like a broken record when you ask God over and over to answer the same request? Do you trust He is in control? Is the stillness weighing on you? Right now, turn the silence into a deeper faith in Jesus. Remember, sometimes in the silence God is doing His most powerful work. Have fun praying, trusting, and praising Jesus in the silence.

MY PRAYER CHAIR
JOURNAL

_____
_____
_____
_____
_____
_____
_____
_____
_____
_____
_____
_____
_____
_____
_____
_____
_____
_____
_____
_____
_____
_____

PRAYER IMPRINT

Far be it from me that I should sin against the Lord by failing to pray for you.

— 1 Samuel 12:23

I will pray for you! How many times have you said these words? Do you actually follow through? Or is it more a conversation statement to make someone feel better? How serious is this phrase to God?

The focus verse for this chapter is 1 Samuel 12:23, *Far be it from me that I should sin against the Lord by failing to pray for you.* Who does Samuel say we sin against when we fail to pray for one another? The Lord! God calls us to pray for each other, lift one another up, and to cry out in prayer for the needs of others. Samuel learned this at an early age. His mother, Hannah, could not conceive a child. She cried out to God for a son, and made a vow to Him...

> *If You will only look on Your servant's misery and remember me, and not forget Your servant but give her a son, then I will give him to the Lord for all the days of his life.*
>
> —1 Samuel 1:11

God heard her cry. He answered her prayer. And she followed through with her promise to Him. The example of Samuel's mother left a prayer imprint on his heart. Throughout the scriptures, we find example after example of Samuel praying for others. I love the fact that when he said he would pray, he did it right then. Like in 1 Samuel 7:5, Samuel said, *Assemble all Israel at Mizpah, and I will intercede with the Lord for you.*

Understanding the importance of following through with "I will pray for you" is only the beginning. Now, do you believe your prayers make a difference? Do you mean what you pray, or do you just say the words out of duty? Get ready to be blown away...

> *Confess your sins to each other and pray for each other so that you may be healed. The prayer of a righteous man is powerful and effective.*
>
> —James 5:16

Pray for each other so that you may be healed? Praying for others heals me? How? The Greek for the word *healed* actually encourages us "to make whole, to free from errors and sins." Wow! When I take time to pray for others, I am affected. A prayer imprint is forever embedded in my heart. My relationship with Jesus deepens. Oh Lord, remind me to pray for others!

I must share an experience I will never forget. A few years ago, I encountered some difficult circumstances as I approached the end of a leadership position. Ready to throw in the towel, I contemplated terminating my commitment early. I asked the Lord for encouragement to finish the race through His strength, not mine.

The next Sunday at church, a woman stopped me in the hall. I knew her name, but didn't really know her personally. The words that came from her mouth penetrated my heart as she asked, "Are you OK? The Lord woke me up at two o'clock in the morning, three nights in a row, to pray for you."

With a shock of wonder, I asked, "What were you praying?" Her answer unlocked the closet of darkness where I hid my pain, anger, and frustration. She said, "For you to hold on! I didn't know what it meant, but I kept praying for you to hold on."

Now I want you to understand a very important point. No one knew of this struggle in my life. And I don't recall ever having a conversation with this person other than a casual greeting before or after church. No one but my husband had a clue of the thoughts occupying my mind. But God, in His infinite way, called this woman, in the middle of the night, to stand in the gap for someone she didn't even know. Her diligence in listening to the Holy Spirit, obeying His call to pray, and then sharing the experience with me is what the Lord used to spur me forward in the last leg of the race. Oh, how thankful I am that she didn't say, "I don't have time. I don't know her. I have to get my beauty sleep!"

PRAYER CHALLENGE

When you tell someone you will pray for them — do it! Follow through with the commitment to pray. In fact, when you tell someone you will pray, do it right then... in the grocery store, on the phone, at work, at church, during exercise class, in the yard. I find if I pray immediately I am more sensitive to the Holy Spirit's nudging to pray again later! It almost becomes a prayer imprint reminding me to follow through with the prayer commitment.

Also, if you awaken in the middle of the night and the Holy Spirit lays someone or a situation on your mind, don't miss the opportunity to stand in the gap. Do it—follow through and pray! By the way, it just might be the sleep aide you need to fall asleep.

MY PRAYER CHAIR
JOURNAL

_____
_____
_____
_____
_____
_____
_____
_____
_____
_____
_____
_____
_____
_____
_____
_____
_____
_____
_____
_____
_____

PRAYER OF PRAISE

Before they call I will answer; while they are still speaking I will hear, says the Lord.

— Isaiah 65:24

How do you respond to answered prayer? Do you quickly lift up a prayer of praise, or do you forget to thank Him? Honestly, it is so easy to keep moving ahead without giving credit where credit is due — to GOD. We get so excited about the answer that sometimes we fail to give our praises and thanksgivings to the Lord.

Let's journey to the Old Testament, 1 Kings 19:1-8, and look at a time in Elijah's life where he failed to lift up a prayer of praise. In

1 Kings 18, Elijah experienced a mountain top miracle. Coming down from the mountain, he came face-to-face with Jezebel — the evil woman who threatened to kill him. Tired, exhausted, and fearful, he ran for his life. After a day's journey into the desert, he sat down under a broom tree and literally prayed to die. He cried out to God, "I have had enough, Lord. Take my life; I am no better than my ancestors."

All of a sudden, an angel touched him and told him to get up. The angel supplied him with food and water. Elijah ate and drank and fell back to sleep. This happened a second time. Looking closely at the scripture, we realize Elijah's prayer was answered immediately. But sadly Elijah didn't recognize or acknowledge God's answer to his prayer. In desperation, he cried out, and God heard him. Elijah's self-absorption didn't allow him to recognize God's provision. He didn't take time to lift a prayer of praise to the Lord!

Is Elijah any different from us today? Many times we cry out to God for help, and in return, He strengthens, provides, encourages, and directs us through our situation. But we fail to recognize Him in the midst of His answers.

I am an accomplisher, one who thrives on marking things off the "To Do" list. In fact, usually my agenda is set days in advance. As a result, when my schedule is interrupted or my house is a wreck, I usually don't respond with a prayer of praise. My flesh takes over, and I allow the situation to run my day rather than focusing on the Lord. It is when I keep my focus on Jesus that my outlook changes.

PRAYER CHALLENGE

Do you recognize God's answers to your prayers? Do you praise Him before you know the answers? Begin asking the Holy Spirit to help you recognize the Lord's work in the midst of your prayers. Ask that your eyes be opened to how and what the Lord is doing. As God answers in His creative and tender ways, remember to lift a prayer of praise to Him. He just might be sending an angel to hand feed you like He did for Elijah!

MY PRAYER CHAIR
JOURNAL

_____
_____
_____
_____
_____
_____
_____
_____
_____
_____
_____
_____
_____
_____
_____
_____
_____
_____
_____
_____

LIFE STOPS

They were forbidden by the Holy Spirit to preach the word in Asia. After they had come to Mysia, they tried to go into Bithynia, but the Spirit did not permit them.

— Acts 16:6-7 (NKJV)

Imagine driving down the road and suddenly, smack dab in the middle of your path, you see a big yellow sign that reads— ROAD CLOSED. Beyond the sign, the road appears to be in good condition. Frustrated and confused, you contemplate going ahead anyway. But you realize you must heed the sign and follow the alternate route. Later you discover why you were halted in your tracks. A few miles past the sign, a bridge collapsed, making the road dangerous and impassable. A sense of relief and thankfulness blankets your whole body as you realize how you were protected.

How do you handle life stops that make no sense at the time? Those in ministry are not immune to life stops. As a speaker, I schedule events months in advance. Due to some unusual circumstances, a large church cancelled an event with me. At first I experienced a disappointment. But a couple of days later, I received a phone call from a woman asking for advice on building a women's ministry team in her church. She acquired my name through an Internet search for "Women's Retreats in Texas." Reflective Life Ministries popped up.

She went on to say that her church was located in a small Texas town with a population of 525, basically in the middle of nowhere. God stirred the hearts of six women to begin a women's ministry, but they had no idea where to start. As we continued to visit, God confirmed in my heart His arrangement of this conversation. God connected us to accomplish His purpose. As a result, she asked me to speak at a kickoff event for the ladies. And wouldn't you know, the only evening that worked in their schedule happened to be the date the other church cancelled. Wow, only God! God allows life stops for a reason. Remember... obey the signs.

The verse at the beginning of this segment, Acts 16:6-7 says, *They were forbidden by the Holy Spirit to preach the word in Asia. After they had come to Mysia, they tried to go into Bithynia, but the Spirit did not permit them.* If you get a chance, read Acts 16: 1-10. Notice who is guiding Paul and Silas — The Holy Spirit — their counselor, teacher, and guide. They followed the Holy Spirit's directions without arguing or complaining! Hmm, a lesson we all need to learn.

PRAYER CHALLENGE

Are you experiencing a life stop? Are you confused and questioning why God is allowing this in your life? Learn to praise Him in the midst of the moment. Thank Him. He knows best and is working out a mighty plan. Praise Him for teaching you to trust Him even though it doesn't seem to make sense. Ask God to prepare you for these unexpected interruptions in your life. Also, take an extra step forward and pray for others who are experiencing life stops. Pray they trust God through it all.

MY PRAYER CHAIR
JOURNAL

_____
_____
_____
_____
_____
_____
_____
_____
_____
_____
_____
_____
_____
_____
_____
_____
_____
_____
_____
_____
_____
_____
_____

PEANUT BUTTER
SANDWICHES

So I opened my mouth, and He (God) gave me the scroll to eat. Then He said to me, "Son of man, eat this scroll I am giving you and fill your stomach with it." So I ate, and it tasted as sweet as honey in my mouth.

—Ezekiel 3:3

It's 5:30 a.m. A loud noise electrifies my body. Without a peep, I reach for the snooze button. Ten minutes later another blast jolts me into motion. With my feet firmly planted on the ground, I make my way to the kitchen. Oh, the blessing of an automatic coffeemaker. Still not fully awake, I notice the clock now reads 5:45 a.m.

A pleading prayer immediately pours out, "Lord, it's another day filled with routines— kids to get ready for school, breakfast to make, dogs to feed, lunches to create, buses to catch, homework to remember, athletic shoes to pack, notes to sign, and whatever else I'm forgetting. And all this has to be done by 6:30 a.m.! Please, help me have a positive attitude this morning."

After waking the children, I take another sip of coffee. I hear a small rumble from the bathroom, which ignites into a roar. What are they fussing about this time? Thankfully my words of wisdom quickly extinguish the argument. Of course, they know from past history it is to their advantage to heed my warning... if you know what I mean.

Cereal is the breakfast of choice—quick and easy! Realizing time is running short, I begin making lunches. In the process, this thought runs through my mind, "How many peanut butter sandwiches have I made over the years?" The minute this thought exits, another idea surfaces, what if I pray for my children as I make their lunches? I can use these peanut butter sandwiches as visual reminders to pray for each one. With a twinge of excitement, I grab the bread, knife, and jars of peanut butter and jelly. With a large glob on my knife, I begin praying...

> "Lord, just as I *spread* this peanut butter on the bread, may You *spread* Your Word on my children's hearts. Give them an excitement to *spread* the message of Jesus to their friends at school. And as this jelly brings *sweetness* to the sandwich, may Your Holy Spirit *sweeten* their relationships with Jesus. Like these two pieces of bread that *cover* the peanut butter and jelly, may Your love and protection *cover* my children's lives.

Finally, as they *eat* these sandwiches, may they experience the *taste* of Your spiritual nourishment throughout their day."

Immediately, I realize God responded to my early morning prayer for a positive attitude. Humbleness fills my heart, soul, and mind. A song of praise comes from my lips as I give God glory for His presence and for answering my prayer.

PRAYER CHALLENGE

Are you in need of a fresh perspective and outlook for the day? Ask the Lord for encouragement throughout your daily routines. Look for ways He spurs you forward and answers your prayers. Oh, how precious it is when we leave the details to Jesus and watch Him change our hearts!

MY PRAYER CHAIR

JOURNAL

_____
_____
_____
_____
_____
_____
_____
_____
_____
_____
_____
_____
_____
_____
_____
_____
_____
_____
_____
_____

WHAT IF...

Do not fear for I am with you; do not be dismayed, for I am your God. I will strengthen you and help you and uphold you with My righteous right-hand.

—Isaiah 41:10

Surely she is not old enough to drive—not the baby of the family. I must admit I'm not ready for this stage in her life. Not that I doubt her ability, but this represents another step closer to independence. With confidence, she secures herself behind the wheel.

A sudden fear jumps into my thoughts. You know the old, "what ifs" that invade your mind like a swarm of bees. What if she doesn't see a car coming towards her? What if she doesn't stop at a red light in time? What if she freezes up while driving? After I catch my breath, the Lord reminds me He is in control. My job is to teach her to be a responsible driver and pray for her safety.

This reminds me of a spiritual life lesson. Often we drive full force throughout the day, and then bam we are sideswiped with unexpected doubts and fears. For example, a mammogram test comes back inconclusive and additional testing is needed. All of a sudden, the "what ifs" attack from every direction, and before we know it, fear replaces our trust in Jesus. This unrest consumes our every thought.

But, what if we changed our thought life into a prayer life? How many thoughts do we have in a day? In my opinion, it must be at least a zillion. What if we changed our thoughts to prayers? How many times would we be communicating with the Lord? We would develop a living, walking, breathing relationship with Jesus.

Do you see the difference? Jesus is the one who refocuses our hearts and minds on Kingdom purposes. Oh, this is such a powerful habit to incorporate into our daily lives. One that changes our lives forever!

PRAYER CHALLENGE

Ask God to help you replace fear with trust. Change your thought life to a prayer life. Meditate on Isaiah 41:10, *Do not fear for I am with you; do not be dismayed for I am your God. I will strengthen you and help you and uphold you with My righteous right-hand.* Does the verse focus on God taking the circumstance away? Does praying automatically remove the situation from your life? No, not at all. God confirms that He is with us in the midst of the circumstance. He wants us to surrender it all to Him, even our fears. Our goal is to exchange the "what ifs" to trust without fear!

MY PRAYER CHAIR

JOURNAL

_____
_____
_____
_____
_____
_____
_____
_____
_____
_____
_____
_____
_____
_____
_____
_____
_____
_____
_____
_____

IN HIS HANDS

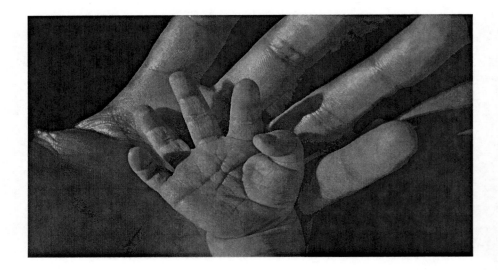

I waited patiently for the Lord; He turned to me and heard my cry.

— Psalm 40:1

Do you feel as if your prayers don't make it past the ceiling? Does it seem like someone hit the mute button when it comes to your prayer life? Are you wondering why God isn't answering your prayers?

Sometimes, in the silence, God is doing His greatest work.

Maybe you are at this point, "I give up! I've prayed for years for this prayer to be answered, but nothing... not a peep, not a word, not a sign, not an answer. I don't think God hears me when I pray!"

When these thoughts seep in, take them captive and place them in the hands of God. We often fasten expectations to our prayers, like how and when we think they need to be answered. When these expectations go unmet, the feelings of disappointment and doubt begin to creep into our minds. Again, with a loud shout I say... take those thoughts captive and place them in the hands of Jesus!

As we pray, God wants us to give Him full access to do His will. For example, in a theater production, do they set up a scene behind the curtain or with the curtain wide open? Usually the curtain is closed or the lights are off. As the curtain opens, the audience jumps right into the scene. Most of the time, we don't even notice the backstage efforts of the crew. This is like God in action. He is always working behind the scenes, so when the curtain opens we enjoy the production.

Read this excerpt from my Bible study, *Reflecting Him: Living for Jesus and Loving It*, Week 7, Day 2...

> In my early adult years, one of my pastors asked me to serve on a committee at church. With excitement and enthusiasm, I said, "Yes." When I walked into the first meeting, I didn't know a soul. After about thirty minutes, I realized one person dominated the conversation, and the more she talked, the more frustrated I became. Thoughts ran through my mind such as, *There is no way I will serve on a team with this person!*
>
> A few days later, without praying, I should add, I decided to withdraw my name from the committee. A sweet Christian friend quietly challenged me to ask the Lord to help me see that person through His eyes. I resolved to pray, but with little expectation of changing my mind.
>
> After a few more meetings, I realized my previous annoyances subsided. Amazingly, God started changing my heart, and I could then view my differences with her as a blessing. I grew to love her because of God's gift of love! You

53

see, the more I tried to control the situation, the more annoyed I became with the committee, and the more frustrated I became with our purpose for serving the Lord. I wanted things to change immediately, but God needed to teach me about waiting on Him. Once I relinquished control over the situation and started praying, God changed me![4]

PRAYER CHALLENGE

Looking at today's photograph, what comes to your mind? Now, read Psalm 40:1 with all of Psalm 5. What do you learn from these verses? Ask God to help you leave your requests in His hands. Trust that He hears your prayers. Believe that He is at work accomplishing His will. If Jesus can leave His circumstances in the hands of God, so can we!

---

[4] McDougal, Carla. Reflecting Him: Living for Jesus and Loving It! (RLMPublishing)145.

MY PRAYER CHAIR
JOURNAL

_____
_____
_____
_____
_____
_____
_____
_____
_____
_____
_____
_____
_____
_____
_____
_____
_____
_____
_____
_____
_____

CRISIS OF BELIEF

But when you ask, you must believe and not doubt, because the one who doubts is like a wave of the sea, blown and tossed by the wind.

—James 1:6

Doubt. Fear. Decisions. Oh, God, what should I do? Have you experienced these thoughts recently? Can you recall a time when you were gripped with fear because of a decision? We have all been there at one time or another. Personally, I would love for God to give me the answer straight up. A billboard sign would be nice. How about an email? Oh, that would work wonderfully! Imagine opening your inbox to see a message from God. Hmm? Why doesn't He work this way?

56

Believers have the privilege to talk to God twenty-four hours a day, seven days a week. He is always there waiting to listen, act, and commune with us. He desires an ongoing communication with His children. If you are a parent you understand. He doesn't want us to call on Him just during emergencies. Oh, He is there during those times we need *crisis counseling*, but He wants us to come to Him for everything.

I remember as a young child hearing my grandmama pray for parking spots at the grocery store. She said sometimes she would get a spot close to the front and other times it was in what she called the boon docks. It didn't matter where she parked. She thanked God for His provision. Her voice still echoes in my heart, "Honey, He is in control." As a child I thought this statement a bit odd. But later I realized she continually displayed an ongoing, daily-seeking, trusting, living relationship with Jesus. What a blessing to watch a woman live her life for Him.

In later years, when her driving days were over, I still called her on a regular basis. When I asked about her day, she often replied with these words, "I'm in my prayer chair!" Tears moisten my cheeks every time I recall her tender, yet powerful words. Grandmama showed me a true picture of what it is to have a daily relationship with Jesus—not based on what I can do for Him, but by being close to Him. I thank God for a grandmama who displayed this living, breathing relationship to her family. I wonder if, in heaven, God replays all the prayers His children prayed? Wow, just thinking about hearing all the prayers my grandmama prayed over me brings me to tears!

PRAYER CHALLENGE

Cuddle up in your Prayer Chair and read James 1:2-6... *Consider it pure joy, my brothers and sisters, whenever you face trials of many kinds, because you know that the testing of your faith produces perseverance. Let perseverance finish its work so that you may be mature and complete. Not lacking anything. If any of you lacks wisdom, you should ask God, who gives generously to all without finding fault, and it will be given to you. But when you ask, you must believe and not doubt, because the one who doubts is like a wave of the sea, blown and tossed by the wind.*

God doesn't want us to just call upon Him for *crisis counseling*. He desires us to come to Him 24/7 with praises, thanks, love, needs, choices, requests for wisdom, and prayers for others. He calls us to an intimate relationship with Himself. Blessings flow when we trust Him!

MY PRAYER CHAIR
JOURNAL

_____
_____
_____
_____
_____
_____
_____
_____
_____
_____
_____
_____
_____
_____
_____
_____
_____
_____
_____
_____
_____
_____

DECISIONS

They all joined together constantly in prayer.
— Acts 1:14

I am so confused! How do I know what to do? Have you ever asked yourself this question? You might be asking it right now. Possibly this image represents your prayers... "Lord, which way should I go?" How do you make the right decisions according to God's will for your life?

Some choices are obvious. If it compromises what God's Word tells us, then the decision is clear. God will never lead us to make a choice that contradicts His Word. Some decisions are a better-best choice. For example, you are offered another job, which involves not only a promotion, but also a location change. This is a great opportunity, but it will be difficult for your high school age children. Your current job offers wonderful benefits, but the chance for advancement is limited. How do you make the right choice? Let's go to the scriptures for the answer.

In Acts 1:15-26, the disciples were faced with a situation. They needed to fill Judas' spot on the team. Peter reminded them of what Psalm 109:8 said, *May his days be few; may another take his place of leadership.*

A challenge to make the right decision lay before them. Two men met the criteria for the position – Joseph called Barsabas and Matthias. Both men were qualified and willing to fill the spot, but only one was God's best for the position. The answer comes in Acts 1:24-25, *And then they prayed, Lord, you know everyone's heart. Show us which one of these two you have chosen to take over this apostolic ministry? Then they cast lots, and the lot fell to Matthias; so he was added to the eleven apostles.*

They prayed, trusting God to show them the best man. They didn't sit around debating about it. They moved forward, seeking the Lord's will. God calls us to pray and move forward in our prayers. What a powerful example of prayer!

We need to act the same today. Bring everything to Jesus. Trust His answer, in His timing, in His way! Pray with boldness when you are faced with making a decision. Trust that God already has the answer. Boldly allow yourself to learn about prayer through the decision making process. Oh, I can hardly contain myself as I am writing these words. God will show you His answer... I promise!

PRAYER CHALLENGE

Faced with a decision? Pray. Now, move forward in God's will as He reveals His plan. Ask the Holy Spirit to remind you to watch for God's answers to your prayers. Never forget to give Him the praise, for the glory belongs to Him!

MY PRAYER CHAIR
JOURNAL

GOT KNEEPADS?

God is our refuge and strength, an ever-present help in trouble
— Psalm 46:1

Driving... every mother's nightmare! Do you remember the first time your child drove out of the driveway — ALONE? No one to remind him to slow down, or point out the fact he is too close to the car ahead of him. A look of independence and accomplishment adorned his face, as well as the dreaded expression of I am invincible. Inwardly, you experienced the bittersweet battles of freedom verses fear — freedom from carpooling children all over town, fear of the freedom your child now has at his disposal.

With three teenage drivers in our home at one time, I needed personalized kneepads. Or maybe I should name them *kneeling pads*. One morning, not three minutes after our third son left for school, I received a phone call. The trembling voice said, "Mom, I hit a deer. Carly knocked her head on the dashboard! I'm on my way back home!" I expected to see the front end of the car smashed, with antlers stuck in the grill. To my amazement, only a small dent was visible.

Tate said, "Mom, I knew I was in trouble when the deer darted towards the road. I know God's angels protected us!" Out of the mouth of a seventeen-year-old boy flowed words of belief in his Savior Jesus. Joy ignited in my heart as I realized God's answer to my prayers. Not only did He protect my children, they experienced God's love through that protection.

PRAYER CHALLENGE

Ask Jesus to help you experience His love and protection. Ask the Lord to open your eyes to the ways God protects you and your family every day. Trust Him with your children in every way. Fear paralyzes, but trust opens the door for you to experience freedom in Christ. *God is our refuge and strength, an ever-present help in trouble.*

—Psalm 46:1

MY PRAYER CHAIR
JOURNAL

_____
_____
_____
_____
_____
_____
_____
_____
_____
_____
_____
_____
_____
_____
_____
_____
_____
_____
_____
_____
_____
_____
_____

LIFE IN THE

FAST LANE

Call to me and I will answer you and tell you great and unsearchable things you do not know, says the Lord.

— Jeremiah 33:3

Busy... Busy-ness... Busy-est! Does this sound familiar? Does this describe your daily life? A few years ago, our two oldest boys came home from college for Easter weekend. After the church service and lunch, our family gathered on the back porch. Stories of the past flooded our conversations. Looking at my eldest son, these words popped out of my mouth, "It seems like yesterday. I can still

66

see your excitement for hunting Easter eggs. Do you remember…?" All of a sudden, this phrase brought back memories of my mom saying the same thing to me.

Why does time seem to move so fast? Do we allow ourselves to get so busy that we lose track of life itself? Does busyness become our enemy? When this happens, many times our prayer life suffers. We hit the ground running in the morning and crawl into bed at night. We become so wrapped up in our own issues and circumstances that each day fades into the next.

As a result, we live to exist. This is not God's plan for us! He desires for us to live every day sold out to Jesus. From the moment we wake up, He is waiting for us to connect with Him. God desires quality time with His children, but He will never push Himself on us. He sets a daily agenda for His children, but it is up to us to pray for the day's assignment!

PRAYER CHALLENGE

Take a break from life in the fast lane, and pray! Right now, take time to ask Him to reveal His agenda for your day. Read Jeremiah 32:16-44 and 33:1-3. Notice how Jeremiah prays for understanding, and God answers. Trust Him in the midst of your prayers. Listen to His tender voice throughout your day.

MY PRAYER CHAIR
JOURNAL

_____

_____

_____

_____

_____

_____

_____

_____

_____

_____

_____

_____

_____

_____

_____

_____

_____

_____

_____

_____

_____

STAND AMAZED

... But my heart stands in awe of Your Word. I rejoice at Your Word as one who finds great treasure.

– Psalm 119:161-162 (NKJV)

The more I read His Word, the more I know Him...

The more I know Him, the more I love Him...

The more I love Him, the more I understand...

Life is not about me, but all about Him!

Do you hear His voice? Can you describe the sound? Is it quiet, gentle, and soft? Or sharp, clear, and decisive?

I must admit my prayers often consist of talking rather than listening. It's almost like a one-sided conversation. You know, the kind that reflects an all about me attitude.

Together let's practice discerning the voice of God. Re-read Psalm 119:161-162. Now let's break it apart...

But my heart stands in awe of Your Word...

When was the last time you stood in awe or amazement at God's word? I don't want to miss one awesome moment of what He is telling me. Asking the Holy Spirit to make each word come alive in our hearts is vital to discerning God's voice. He brings freshness to spiritual truths in God's Word.

I rejoice at Your Word as one who finds great treasure...

As the ultimate teacher and counselor, the Holy Spirit constantly points us to Jesus. Convicting. Revealing truths. Communicating wisdom. Ask for a heart of understanding and look for spiritual treasures. God lavishes His love on us through His Word. Praise God for intimate moments with the Savior!

Have you experienced God's majesty? A few years ago, I asked the Lord to reveal His majesty to me. I basically hid this prayer in the crevices of my heart. Later in the week, I went shopping with a friend who recently accepted Jesus into her life. In the midst of a great time, I happened to look upward into the sky. My mouth dropped open as I viewed the most magnificent sight, one I'd never seen before. A vivid rainbow encircled the sun! Each color glistened with radiance, intensity, and brilliance as if to sing, "Majesty, Stand Amazed at His Glory!" I almost fell to my knees, praising God in the parking lot. Amazement adorned my face as I shared with my friend the request I prayed earlier that week.

God, in all His glory, chose to answer my request in a unique and personal way. As a result, not only did I have a tender moment with God's majesty, but my new sister-in-Christ experienced God's splendor as well. I learned a vital lesson that day. Almost as if God audibly spoke to me saying, "Carla, when you ask Me to reveal Myself to you, keep your eyes open for the ways in which I choose to make Myself known. I just might use your prayer to reveal My majesty and glory to others around you." What a sweet and tender moment, one I will never forget.

The more I read His Word, the more I know Him...

The more I know Him, the more I love Him...

The more I love Him, the more I understand...

Life is not about me, but all about Him!

PRAYER CHALLENGE

Read Psalm 119:161-176. If possible, read this passage in the New King James Version. Notice how many times the psalmist uses *Your Word, Your law, Your testimony, Your salvation, Your commands, Your statutes, Your judgments,* and *Your precepts.* The psalmist doesn't rebel against God's ways, but instead affirms his love, dedication, and trust in the Lord. How powerful! Ask the Lord to open your eyes to His Word so that you completely understand His grace and mercy of salvation through His son, Jesus. Commit to reading God's Word every day. Then watch for His teaching moments throughout the day. Stand amazed with your walking, talking, breathing relationship with Jesus.

MY PRAYER CHAIR
JOURNAL

_____
_____
_____
_____
_____
_____
_____
_____
_____
_____
_____
_____
_____
_____
_____
_____
_____
_____
_____
_____
_____
_____

Dog Days of
Summer

The Lord will roar from Zion and thunder from Jerusalem; the earth and the sky will tremble. But the Lord will be a refuge for His people, a stronghold for the people of Israel.

—Joel 3:16

What comes to mind when you hear the term "dog days of summer"? Many times this phrase is used to describe the hot, dry summer months. Maybe your thoughts drift to your childhood when the sounds of locusts lulled you to sleep. Possibly you recall a scorching wind blowing in your face or walking barefoot in the heat of the day. The minute your feet touched the blistering pavement you started the sidewalk dance. This unique jig continued until your feet landed in the shade or in the grass.

God uses real life situations to teach us spiritual life lessons. For example, the weather affects not only our physical bodies, but also our emotions and spiritual conditions. Re-read Joel 3:16 above. Now read Isaiah 25:1,4... *O Lord, You are my God. I will exalt You, I will praise Your name, For You have done wonderful things... For You have been a shelter from the storm and a shade from the heat. (NKJV)*

The Sun is vital to our human existence. As the Sun emits visible light, heat, and ultraviolet rays, the human body experiences the Sun's impact. It is easy to see how visible light affects us. Ultraviolet light is unseen by the human eye and not felt by the human body, but its effects on a body's health are far reaching. In fact, some of its most essential health benefits go unnoticed. For example, one of the greatest advantages of ultraviolet light is the production of Vitamin D. This vitamin is essential to calcium metabolism, the formation of bone growth, and fighting skin diseases. In the northern regions of the world, the Sun only shines a few hours a day throughout the winter. During this time of darkness, people are prone to depression. One reason for this disorder is a deficiency of Vitamin D.

Isn't this like the Christian life? There are times when God allows us to view glimpses of His mighty hand of healing, peace, judgment, protection, etc. At other times, we experience the heat of situations and circumstances in life that need purification. Yet behind the scenes, the Lord is continuously accomplishing His purposes. God is daily injecting doses of spiritual vitamins, which our souls need to overcome sinful diseases that work to invade our thoughts, hearts, and lives. Many times we are unaware of these expressions of God's love that are so vital to sustaining our spiritual health.

Are you experiencing some dog days in your personal life... marriage, children, illness, work, finances, commitments, relationships, responsibilities, or decisions? Is the heat of a situation zapping your spiritual energy? God calls us to do the sidewalk dance and run to Him, so we can abide under the shadow of the Almighty. Prayer keeps us under the shelter of His wings.

PRAYER CHALLENGE

Read Psalm 63 and Psalm 91. Write a personal prayer about your own "dog days of summer" and ask God to be your continual shade from the heat! Praise Him for the unseen things He is doing in and through your life. Ask Him to open your eyes to recognize His hand of protection, love, purpose, grace, and mercy. At the same time, pray for others experiencing their own heated circumstances. Just a thought—you might be the only one praying over their situations. Lifting others up is a privilege given to believers by God Himself. What an honor!

MY PRAYER CHAIR
JOURNAL

_____
_____
_____
_____
_____
_____
_____
_____
_____
_____
_____
_____
_____
_____
_____
_____
_____
_____
_____
_____
_____

JUST BREATHE

Praise be to the Lord, for he has heard my cry for mercy. The Lord is my strength and my shield; my heart trusts in him and He helps me. My heart leaps for joy and with my song I praise Him.

— Psalm 28:6-7

Scattered? Pulled in every direction? Agenda set days in advance? Craving to just breathe? Today's society lives in the fast lane. At the touch of a button, things shift into motion... the snooze alarms, preset coffee makers, instant microwave breakfasts, automatic door openers, MP3 players loaded with thousands of songs (Remember the eight-track tape players? You waited at least four songs to hear your favorite!), DVRs for the televisions, and the list goes on and on. This technology age opened the doors to a whole new world of conveniences, but also a whole new set of expectations.

In many ways, we've lost the ability to practice patience. Spending time with God has become more like the drive through lane at a fast-food restaurant. We quickly place our order, drive up to the window, pay the cashier, receive the food, and drive off. We even get frustrated if the line is too long! By the time we arrive at the window, our attitudes sometimes don't display appreciation, but annoyance.

Recently a friend joined me on a trip to Michigan where I was the speaker for a large retreat. She and I live in different towns in Texas, so we decided to meet at the airport in Grand Rapids. After renting a car and securing the destination on our GPS, we were on our way. Our excitement filled the car with laughter, conversation, and joy! My friend needed a little nourishment, so we pulled into a fast-food line to get her a hamburger and soft drink.

After placing the order, I drove up to the first window, paid for the food, and then proceeded to the next window to pick it up. Now, you must know this before I continue. She and I hadn't stopped talking or laughing since we got in the car. So, without thinking, I just drove right past the second window. I was in the parking lot when my friend screamed, "Carla, you forgot my food!" Putting on the brakes, I looked in the rearview mirror and could see the fast-food worker frantically waving her arms and holding the bag out the window. I put the car in reverse, backed up, and accepted the bag from the woman who just rolled her eyes at me. Needless to say, my friend and I still laugh about the incident today!

Unfortunately, we are often careless with the way we treat God, although we want Him to answer our requests immediately, in our time, and on our schedule. If He makes us wait, we get frustrated, discontented, and displeased. We plead with Him on behalf of our immediate needs and then fail to grasp His response. At times when we pray, we are so busy with our own agendas we drive right past God as He is trying to hand us the answer.

Oh, how many times do we miss Jesus in the midst of our days? If only we would take the time to just breathe and refocus on Him. Developing moment-by-moment communication with our Savior inspires a living, walking, breathing relationship with Jesus.

We must ask ourselves these questions. What are we teaching our children and our grandchildren? Are we missing God's miracles for our families and ourselves? Is this fast-paced life developing self-centered individuals rather than God-centered people?

PRAYER CHALLENGE

Please re-read today's verse—Psalm 28:6-7. Before reading, just breathe. Ask the Holy Spirit to open your heart to a fresh truth. Just breathe once again. Notice how many times God says, "I will..." What is He saying to you? Close your eyes and just breathe. God loves you. God calls you into righteousness. God is holding your hand. God is keeping you! Open your arms to the heavens and just breathe a sigh of humbleness to the Father who created and stretched out the heavens. Recognize Jesus in your everyday life. Relax for a moment and just breathe Him in. As oxygen is to the blood, so is the Holy Spirit to your spiritual walk.

MY PRAYER CHAIR
JOURNAL

_____
_____
_____
_____
_____
_____
_____
_____
_____
_____
_____
_____
_____
_____
_____
_____
_____
_____
_____
_____

EXERCISE YOUR PRAYER LIFE

Ask and it will be given to you; seek and you will find; knock and the door will be opened to you. For everyone who asks receives, and to him who knocks, the door will be opened.

– Matthew 7:7-8

Have you taken time to pray today? Did you wake up with thoughts of Jesus on your heart, mind, and soul? He is waiting every morning for our first thoughts to be on Him, praising Him for who He is, what He has done, for how He works all things to His glory.

So often when the alarm goes off, we hit the snooze button a few times. Frequently this leads to the "Late Again Syndrome." We fly out of bed and rush to accomplish the morning's activities. All the while, Jesus is on the back burner of our minds. He never pushes Himself on us, although He desires for His children to seek Him, search the Word, sing praises to His name, and call upon the name of the Lord in all things.

How does regular exercise benefit our ability to breathe? When we exercise on a regular basis, our lung capacity increases, allowing a larger volume of air to enter our lungs. High intensity workouts require deep breathing, which in turn causes the lungs to increase air intake. This is beneficial for everyone because an increased lung capacity not only enhances our stamina, but it is good for our overall health. A larger lung capacity and increased oxygen level help circulate blood in the body. A better blood flow aids in cleansing the veins and arteries. So, increased lung capacity = increased oxygen intake = increased blood flow = blood and vein cleansing!

How does spiritual exercise benefit our spiritual breathing? By now you know I love to use real-life lessons as a way to teach spiritual truths. So here goes. As long as we are alive, we breathe air, and we know there are ways to improve our breathing capacity. We can do the same with our spiritual breathing. The more time we spend with Jesus, the more we enhance our intake of the Holy Spirit. The minute we become alive in Christ, the Holy Spirit resides inside us forever. And when we desire to live a life sold out to Jesus—walking in the Spirit and not in the flesh—we increase our spiritual lung capacity. The deeper we breathe in the Holy Spirit, the more we allow Him to flow through us. He cleanses our lives of impurities. As we breathe Him in, we experience fulfillment of His presence. He gives us the yearning to exercise a prayer life with Him, stay fit through Bible study, and work out our daily problems through Him.

Wow, increased time with Jesus =

> Increased spiritual understanding =

>> Increased Holy Spirit flow =

>>> Spiritual cleansing!

PRAYER CHALLENGE

Seek Jesus first in the morning before your head ever leaves the pillow. Commune with Him at the dawning of your day. Need a reminder? Ask the Holy Spirit for an inward nudge to seek the Lord first thing every morning. Then watch to see how your day unfolds. It is so much fun to have a personal relationship with Jesus — King of kings, Lord of lords, Savior of the World.

MY PRAYER CHAIR
JOURNAL

_____
_____
_____
_____
_____
_____
_____
_____
_____
_____
_____
_____
_____
_____
_____
_____
_____
_____
_____

IN HARMONY

Therefore, be alert and of sober mind so that you can pray. Above all, love each other deeply, because love covers a multitude of sins.

–1 Peter 4:7-8

In the quiet of your heart, can you hear the orchestra? The richness of sounds blended into one? A symphony has the ability to lull a crying baby or bring calm in the midst of a storm. Many times when played alone, instruments sound out of tune or off key. But when played together, they create beautiful harmony, each musical instrument complimenting the other. The music inspires, soothes, and even mesmerizes the soul.

1 Peter 3:8 says, *All of you live in harmony with one another.* This word *harmony* in the Greek means of "one mind, one passion." This is actually a combination of two words, which gives the idea of rushing along, together in unison. Like with music, a number of notes played at the same time are different, but harmonize in pitch and tone. They captivate the audience from the first note.

This is a picture of the body of Christ when we are of one mind. As a famous concertmaster directs the symphony, so the Holy Spirit blends together the prayers of the saints. God desires for His children to pray together and make beautiful music through their prayers.

I love that 1 Peter 3:12 says, *For the eyes of the Lord are on the righteous and His ears are attentive to their prayer.* As the leader of the first church in Acts, Peter grasped the importance of coming together to lift praises and requests to the Lord. We should live out this example in our own lives.

Why do we make corporate prayer a last resort? Over and over, God's Word gives us examples of believers coming together to pray, and God answering those prayers. God calls us to pray! This is exciting. God gives us an opportunity to participate in eternity with Him, through prayer.

At the end of one of my speaking engagements, a woman waited until most of the ladies left the venue. With slumped shoulders and a whisper to her voice, she asked if she could visit with me for a few minutes. I said, "Of course!" In our conversation she opened a dark closet of her soul—a place she'd hidden for years. Grabbing her hands, I asked if I could pray with her, and she agreed. A sweet union immediately formed. The harmony of that prayer still plays in my heart.

A few weeks later I received an email from her. She explained how sharing her dark secret opened the door to freedom. The chains that once held her captive were broken. She went on to say when I was praying with her, she literally experienced that dark area being filled with the Light—Jesus. Prayer opened the door for freedom from the dungeon of despair.

Praise God for the blessings of corporate prayer. Let's pray together! Don't miss the blessings of drawing nearer to God and other believers as you create beautiful prayer melodies together.

PRAYER CHALLENGE

Please read 1 Peter 3:8-12 and 1 Peter 4:1-12. Ask the Lord to lead you to a group of believers you can pray with on a regular basis. If you are afraid to step out in this way, ask God for courage. When you need prayer for a situation, ask Him to direct you to one or more prayer warriors. Oh, the harmony of the saints coming together blesses the soul!

MY PRAYER CHAIR
JOURNAL

_____
_____
_____
_____
_____
_____
_____
_____
_____
_____
_____
_____
_____
_____
_____
_____
_____
_____
_____
_____
_____

WAKE-UP CALL

And pray in the Spirit on all occasions with all kinds of prayers and requests. With this in mind, be alert and always keep on praying for all the saints.

—Ephesians 6:18

It's the middle of the night. The phone isn't ringing. Darkness fills the room. Children are nestled in their beds. All is quiet. So, why am I still awake?

Frustrated. Exhausted. I must turn off my thoughts. But my mind continues replaying the conversations and events of the day as well as the things I need to do tomorrow.

Why am I still awake? "Come on, fall asleep," I tell myself. My busy days require so much energy. Anger kindles. I can't go through the day with only a few hours of sleep.

Why am I still awake? All of a sudden, a thought flashes through my mind, "Is the Holy Spirit giving me a wake-up call to pray?" In no time flat, a friend's circumstances flash through my mind. At the same time, I recall Ephesians 6:18, *And pray in the Spirit on all occasions with all kinds of prayers and requests. With this in mind, be alert and always keep on praying for all the saints.* Prayers ignite. This tender moment with the Holy Spirit changed my life forever. Why? Because this experience taught me to be alert and prepared to stand in the gap for others at any moment. Oh, the intimacy of a personal relationship with Jesus continues to bring me to my knees!

The Old Testament is filled with spiritual wake-up calls. For example, God warned the Israelites of the destruction ahead of them if they didn't change their hearts and repent. Many times God used prophets to proclaim His message. For example, Jeremiah 1:5 where God comes to Jeremiah and says, *Before I formed you in the womb I knew you, before your were born I set you apart; I appointed you as a prophet to the nations.*

God called Jeremiah to be His voice as a warning to the Israelites about God's judgment upon His people and the coming destruction of the land. Over and over Jeremiah warned the Israelites to turn from their wicked ways.

We see God's warnings all around us. They are directed not only to us personally, but to our nation. The moral decay in America continues to spread. God is sending His wake-up calls all around us. We must pray for our nation to turn back to Jesus.

PRAYER CHALLENGE

The next time you wake up in the middle of the night, ask the Holy Spirit to place a person or a situation on your heart. Pray right then. You might be the only one God calls to stand in the gap.

MY PRAYER CHAIR
JOURNAL

_____

_____

_____

_____

_____

_____

_____

_____

_____

_____

_____

_____

_____

_____

_____

_____

_____

_____

_____

DO NOT ENTER

Live by the Spirit, and you will not gratify the desires of the sinful nature. For the sinful nature desires what is contrary to the Spirit, and the Spirit what is contrary to the sinful nature. They are in conflict with each other, so that you do not do what you want.

— Galatians 5:16-17

Do Not Enter... Do Not Disturb... Keep Off! What is it about human nature? Why do we want to do things we shouldn't? The battle against right and wrong constantly plagues our minds.

Think about this... You're late for a job interview. Pulling into the parking lot, you notice an open spot close to the front of the building. A sigh of relief comes over you. As you park, you notice the beautiful landscape bridging the gap between you and the entrance. Your eyes focus on a large sign, commanding pedestrians to KEEP OFF!

Decision time. If you follow the sidewalk, you have to walk all the way around the pristine, grassy garden area. You look around, don't see anyone, and say to yourself, "Oh, well." Justifying your decision, you tiptoe through the manicured area. Relieved, you smile and walk through the entrance. During the appointment, the interviewer casually mentions he noticed you getting out of your car. In a split second your face reads, "Guilty as charged!"

Remember Adam and Eve in Genesis 3? God offered them the freedom to eat from any tree in the garden except one... the Tree of the Knowledge of Good and Evil (Gen. 2:17). God put an imaginary sign on this tree that said DO NOT EAT THE FRUIT. Well, we know Adam watched his wife, Eve, yield to Satan's temptation. Both ate from the tree, and immediately sin entered the world. If only she heeded the warning!

Are we any different from Adam and Eve? For example, a toddler is told over and over not to touch a hot stove, but he defies the command and does it anyway. The pain reminds him next time to listen to the voice of warning. Living by the Spirit gives us the strength to reject the desire to gratify the flesh.

Prayer is the key to living in the Spirit and not in the flesh. Prayer keeps us in continual communication with Jesus and more aware of the Holy Spirit's direction in our daily lives.

PRAYER CHALLENGE

Is God placing any warning signs before you? How does He want you to respond? What are some things you can do to obey the "Keep Off" and "Do Not Enter" notifications? Read all of Gal. 5:16-26. Remember, God knows what is best for us, but He doesn't make us obey. Obedience is a choice. I can't help but wonder if God smiles, claps His hands, and shouts, "Yes!" when we heed His warning signs. Obedience is a choice worth making!

MY PRAYER CHAIR
JOURNAL

_____
_____
_____
_____
_____
_____
_____
_____
_____
_____
_____
_____
_____
_____
_____
_____
_____
_____

NEVER-ENDING
LAUNDRY

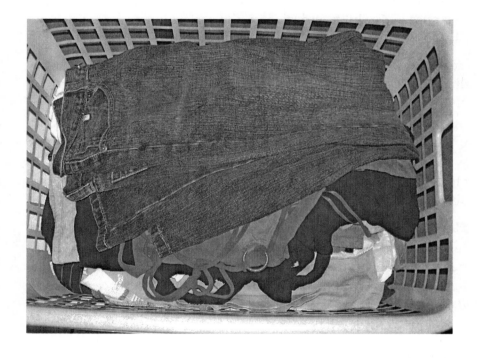

So, whether you eat or drink or whatever you do, do it all for the glory of God.

— 1 Corinthians 10:31

Laundry... the never-ending household chore. As children get older, the laundry piles grow exponentially. These mounds represent daily outfits, workout clothes, multiple single socks, towels, friend's clothes that somehow end up in the mix, and more. The minute the clothes are washed, dried, folded, and put in their proper places, another mound lurks from within the hamper. In all honesty, sometimes I want to throw in the towel when it comes to this job.

The anonymous "Single-Sock Mystery" hits every household. I haven't met anyone yet who hasn't tried to solve it. Somewhere between the laundry bin, the washer, and the dryer — socks just disappear. My children decided if the sock colors sort of match, it's okay to wear them.

Years ago I read a book challenging me to change my daily mommy chores into mommy prayers. As a result, I began praying for my children as I wiped noses, changed diapers, potty trained, prepared meals, filled bottles, washed clothes and hands, and more. For example, instead of focusing on the dirty clothes that needed washing, I started praying for the child who wore the clothes. This change of heart and attitude produced a fresh excitement to accomplish all the mommy tasks.

How do we persevere through our daily routines? What can we do to make each moment count for the Kingdom of God? Even the never-ending laundry saga is an opportunity to draw nearer to Jesus. How? By putting 1 Cor. 10:31 into action, ...*whatever you do, do it for the glory of God.*

PRAYER CHALLENGE

Turn your daily chores into prayers. Begin with the never-ending laundry pile. As you fold each *piece* of clothing, pray for the *peace* of God to fill the heart of the person who wears it. Have fun as you do everything for the glory of the Lord.

MY PRAYER CHAIR
JOURNAL

_____
_____
_____
_____
_____
_____
_____
_____
_____
_____
_____
_____
_____
_____
_____
_____
_____
_____
_____
_____

God's Love Story

From the Mother
of the Groom

I will greatly rejoice in the Lord, my soul shall be joyful in my God. For He has clothed me with the garments of salvation, He has covered me with the robe of righteousness. As a bridegroom decks himself with ornaments, and as a bride adorns herself with her jewels.

— Isaiah 61:10 (NKJV)

Anticipation intensifies. The guests rise in silence. All eyes focus intently on the chapel doors. Beads of sweat form on my son's forehead. His heartbeat escalates with each passing second. Glancing at me, he gives a quick love wink. Within seconds, I feel my betrothed of twenty-eight years grasp my hand. His gentle touch calms the nerves surging through my body.

Within seconds, flashbacks of my son's life flood my mind. Faded memories seem like yesterday. For twenty-six years I prayed for this very moment. Deep within, a tender praise ignites, "Thank you, God! She is the bride you picked for our son. They both love you with all their hearts, minds, souls, and strength. Their purity is a picture of Your design for marriage. Bless this covenant of marriage, this union between You and Your children. " Tears of joy cascade down. Contentment captivates me like never before.

The music fills the sanctuary. Anxious hearts anticipate the bride's entrance. Heads oscillate back and forth between the groom at the front of the chapel and the doors at the back. The song begins its crescendo. The doors slowly open and there, standing before the bridegroom, is his bride.

I quickly gaze back at my son. To my amazement, I catch a glimpse of the image of Jesus as the bridegroom waiting for His bride, the church. My son's look of anticipation reminds me of Christ's return and His love for the church. A snapshot forever imprinted on my heart. A thankful heart connects my soul to God.

With each step the bride narrows the gap between her and her beloved. For a brief moment, tears distort my son's vision. His heartbeat plays a love song for her only. The bride's father places her hand in my son's palm. An immediate rush of joy overwhelms the onlookers. God's love envelops the couple. God's presence overwhelms the guests. His blessings pour out in the midst of this covenant ordained by Him.

All at once, I recall Song of Solomon 1:15, *Behold, you are beautiful, my love! Behold, you are beautiful. You have the eyes of a dove.* I sense my son's love, desire, and commitment for his pure, innocent, and beautiful bride. I am captivated by God's love story being displayed. I sense Jesus proclaiming to the guests, *Behold, you are beautiful, my love! Behold, you are beautiful...* My heart pounds, and once again tears well up.

Finally, a kiss seals the covenant, and the pastor presents Mr. and Mrs. Luke McDougal. Running hand-in-hand down the aisle, the couple's joy shines brightly. Showers of blessings fall from heaven. God's love story washes over all who witnessed this pledge between a man of God, his bride, and God — the Father, Son, and Holy Spirit.

PRAYER CHALLENGE

Begin praying for God to unite your child or grandchild with His chosen spouse. I started praying for their mates while my children were still in the womb. I asked God to draw this special one to Himself and for Him to prepare each for the other. As parents, our goal is to raise our children to love Jesus with all their hearts, souls, minds, and strength. Pray for them to choose a helpmate who has a passion and love for Jesus. It is so much fun watching God puzzle their lives together.

MY PRAYER CHAIR
JOURNAL

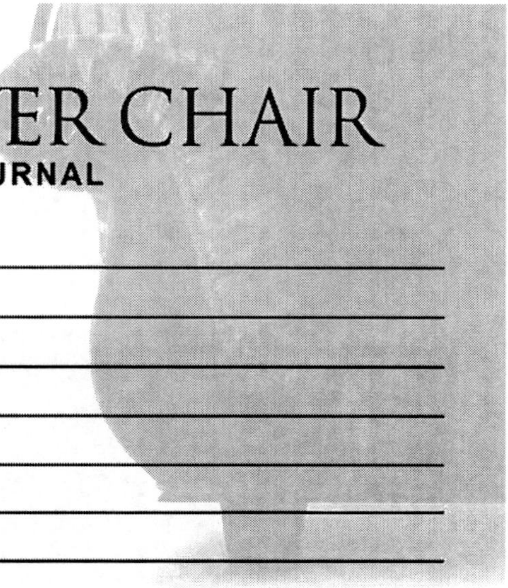

_____

_____

_____

_____

_____

_____

_____

_____

_____

_____

_____

_____

_____

_____

_____

_____

_____

_____

_____

_____

_____

_____

THE NEW NORMAL

He put a new song in my mouth, a hymn of praise to our God.
Many will see and fear and put their trust in the Lord.

— Psalm 40:3

Fear of the unknown steals my joy. My out of control thoughts mimic fireworks on the Fourth of July. Waking from a restless sleep, I wonder what this next season holds. Before my eyes see the dawning light, a prayer ignites...

"Lord, this is my new normal. I don't want to miss a moment of what you have planned. Thank you for the blessings of raising our children. As they embark on their new normals, protect them and draw them to Yourself. Help them love you with all their hearts, souls, minds, and strength. May we all embrace this new normal with excitement and expectations as Your plans unfold. Amen."

Silence fills every room. The absence of noise creates a sweet, quiet time with Jesus. Streams of requests pour from the depths of my soul. This tender communion deposits deeper trust in Him. Embracing this new normal creates a river of hope. In an instant, a hint of joy springs forth. But the ever-present fear of the unknown lingers throughout the day. My prayer hotline to the Father activates my surrendered heart. Again I cry out, "Oh Lord, please help me adjust to this new normal!"

As the day fades into evening, a thought kindles. The genre of soft jazz sets the stage for transforming our living room into a romantic ballroom. Looking at my husband, I ask him for a dance. Without a word he jumps to his feet and draws me to himself. His embrace captivates my heart like never before. All of a sudden, these words pour in—*You are his and he is yours. You get to spend the rest of your life together! This is the beginning of your new normal.* Tears well up. Heart pounds. Joy overflows!

My answered prayer came wrapped in the gift of a dance. I thank my Heavenly Father for this new normal. I praise Him for answering my prayers and showing me His fresh perspective.

PRAYER CHALLENGE

If you are on the horizon of a new normal, ask the Lord to show you a glimpse of His plan. Don't miss a minute of this fresh season. His purposes far outweigh our expectations. And remember, fear of the unknown robs our joy and steals our peace. Enjoy the journey of your new normal.

MY PRAYER CHAIR
JOURNAL

_____
_____
_____
_____
_____
_____
_____
_____
_____
_____
_____
_____
_____
_____
_____
_____
_____
_____
_____

SHOOTING STARS

When I consider Your heavens, the work of Your fingers, the moon and the stars, which You have set in place, what is man that You are mindful of him, the son of man that You care for him.

—Psalm 8:3,4

Do you recall the first time you witnessed a shooting star? Were you amazed, stunned, excited, or confused? I remember lying in the grass as a child, gazing into a night sky just waiting for a star to zip through the galaxy. It seemed the longer I stared, the closer each star appeared. Occasionally I would catch a glimpse of light streaming its way through the darkness. Excitement filled me.

Wonder overwhelmed me. A moment of God's splendor forever embedded in my heart.

Together let's look at God's Word. Meditate on Habakkuk 3:4, *His splendor was like the sunrise; rays flashed from His hand, where His power was hidden.* By God's hand, the foundations of the Earth were formed. His hand spread out the heavens, and rays flashed from His hand, where His power was hidden. What power was hidden?

In Genesis 1:26, God said, *Let Us make man in Our image, according to Our likeness.* From this we know Jesus and the Holy Spirit were with God at the time of creation. Then in John 8:12 Jesus says, *I am the light of the world. He who follows Me shall not walk in darkness, but have the light of life.*

Think with me for a minute. Could it be the power that went out from God's hand to be the light of the world was Jesus? Picture God opening His hand so Jesus is released to pass quickly through the universe and embed Himself in the womb of a young girl named Mary. The Light of the World was concealed in the darkness of the womb until He came into this world as a baby. In that moment, a star appeared in the eastern sky as a spotlight on the arrival of the long-awaited Messiah. Oh, recognize the active hand of God in your life today and allow Him to be the Light of your life!

This reminds me of our spiritual lives. The more we focus on the Lord, the closer we sense His presence in our lives. How many times do we miss God's majestic night light display because we are too busy to look up? Focusing on the things of this world causes us to miss God's tender hand of grace and mercy.

PRAYER CHALLENGE

Prayer is the key to staying focused on Jesus so you don't miss a moment of His presence in your life. Read Psalm 8:3-4, *When I consider your heavens, the work of your fingers, the moon and the stars, which you have set in place, what is man that you are mindful of him, the son of man that you care for him?* Write this verse on a piece of paper. Put it in a strategic place as a reminder of His hand on your life every day. Jesus loves you so much, and He desires a daily relationship with you. Never forget He is the *Bright and Morning Star* (Revelation 22:16).

MY PRAYER CHAIR
JOURNAL

_____
_____
_____
_____
_____
_____
_____
_____
_____
_____
_____
_____
_____
_____
_____
_____
_____
_____
_____
_____
_____

DIVERSIONS

But Martha was distracted by all the preparations that had to be made. She came to him and asked, "Lord, don't you care that my sister has left me to do the work by myself? Tell her to help me!"
— Luke 10:40

In the middle of rush hour traffic, I noticed a mosquito buzzing around my head. Already frustrated from my hectic day, I come to a screeching halt at a red light. Yes, this is my chance to seize the pest.

All of a sudden, the pesky varmint started using my head for target practice. He'd build up speed and dive right at my ear. So, I waved my hands in the air trying to swat the thing. No luck. Then I'd take another whack close to my ear, but still no success. Finally, I see him buzzing right in front of my face. This is my moment of victory. I feel it. With eagerness and determination, I quickly smack my hands together and claim the victory. I wave my fist into the air and say, "Yes, I got you!"

Then it happened. I glanced over at the car next to me and noticed a strange look on the woman's face. In no time flat, her facial expression changed from a sour look to laughter.

Embarrassed, I smiled and waved before turning my head. A smirk emerged just thinking about the incident. Prior to this mosquito moment my attitude was negative and cranky. But this diversion opened the door for a different outlook to my day.

Driving away from the scene, a thought emerged. Maybe, somehow, this experience brought a smile to that person and anyone else who observed my actions. In fact, I started praying for God to use my situation to bring the driver joy. It may sound funny to pray for something so trivial, but I believe God uses life experiences to remind us to keep focused on Him no matter what the situation.

PRAYER CHALLENGE

Look for the diversions the Lord uses to bring a smile to your face. Ask Him to remind you to stay focused on Him, so you keep things in perspective. When experiencing a bad day, look for how God provides ways to move you from focusing on the situation to looking for Him through the situation.

On the flip side, you might be the one God uses to help someone make it through her day. Let's say you are checking out at the grocery store. The cashier has a sour look on her face as she scans your groceries. You are faced with a choice—you can respond back with an unpleasant attitude, or you can pray for her, smile, and give her a positive word of encouragement. You might be the diversion God uses to move her from focusing on herself to thinking about Jesus.

MY PRAYER CHAIR
JOURNAL

_____
_____
_____
_____
_____
_____
_____
_____
_____
_____
_____
_____
_____
_____
_____
_____
_____
_____
_____

SPIRITUAL CONGESTION

Blessed is he whose transgressions are forgiven, whose sins are covered. Blessed is the man whose sin the Lord does not count against him and in whose spirit is no deceit.

— Psalm 32:1,2

Suffering through the common, seasonal cold brings headaches, sleepless nights, and overall physical frustration. Clogged nasal passages make it difficult to breathe, and a side effect is that you might lose your sense of smell. Can you relate to this temporary, but frustrating condition?

One evening I was home alone suffering with a cold. I let our dog inside to keep me company. A few hours later my children walked into the house and immediately started yelling, "Mom, what is that awful smell? It smells like a skunk!" To my dismay, our protective canine must have wrestled with a skunk in the backyard. Guess who won the fight! Because of my cold, I couldn't detect the pungent odor right under my nose. I did wonder why he was rubbing his body all over the rugs in the house. But I just thought he needed to scratch his back. Needless to say, the smell lingered for days and days.

God created humans with the amazing ability to detect thousands of odors. This automatic sense of smell, called the olfactory system, is constantly activated in our bodies. Because of this high level of sensitivity, we are able to distinguish between smells that draw us to the source, as well as odors that cause us to run away.

In biblical times, sweet perfumes and odors were used to reflect triumphs and victories. Conversely, there were fragrances that represented death. Notice what 2 Cor. 2:14 says, *But thanks be to God, who always leads us as captives in Christ's triumphal procession and uses us to spread the aroma of the knowledge of Him everywhere.* Paul used the Roman triumphal procession as a figure of speech to praise God. In a victory procession, the priests followed the Roman general with vessels filled with incense. This presented the spectators with a smell of victory over the enemy.

Paul, of course, presented God as the conquering general leading the victory parade. He and the others who preached about Jesus released the sweet fragrance of victory in Christ. The name *Jesus* in the Greek means "the anointed one, salvation, Messiah." In other words, His anointing is a sweet aroma that penetrates everything

116

and everyone. As Jesus indwells believers, His fragrance seeps out from us to those we encounter.

PRAYER CHALLENGE

Do you see a correlation between physical congestion and spiritual congestion? When we allow sin to invade our lives, it's like our heads being plugged up with colds. In either case, it's difficult to breathe clearly. Confessing sin is like taking a decongestant. It relieves the effects sin has on our lives. Today, take time to confess to the Lord any areas of sin, so you can inhale the sweet aroma of Jesus! Read all of Psalm 32, The Joy of Forgiveness.

MY PRAYER CHAIR
JOURNAL

_____

_____

_____

_____

_____

_____

_____

_____

_____

_____

_____

_____

_____

_____

_____

_____

_____

_____

_____

SPIRITUAL INDIGESTION

At that time the disciples came to Jesus and asked, "Who is the greatest in the kingdom of heaven?" He called a little child and had him stand among them. And he said: "I tell you the truth, unless you change and become like little children, you will never enter the kingdom of heaven. Therefore, whoever humbles himself like this child is the greatest in the kingdom of heaven. And whoever welcomes a little child like this in my name welcomes Me."

—Matthew 18:1-5

To understand Spiritual Indigestion, you must first read Spiritual Congestion. Please take a look at the sweet, innocent face of our dog, Javorski. He gently loves on his babies (stuffed animals) while he sleeps. I know there is a sweet tender feeling welling up inside as you look at this precious, calm, and submissive member of our family, right? Wrong!

One night our family decided to play a card game. It required five dollars per person for an entry fee. Luke, the dealer, put the money on the floor. When the game ended, Carly was the big winner. Luke reached down to retrieve her winnings, but the twenty-dollar bill was gone. We searched everywhere—on the floor, in and under the furniture, all over the room. Puzzled, we retraced our steps. All the while, Javorski casually lounged beneath the table. The mystery continued until Jake exclaimed, "I think Javorski ate the money!"

Words spewed out like "No way. That's crazy. Javorski wouldn't eat a twenty-dollar bill!"

Then Jake pulled out another bill from his wallet and gently tossed it in Javorski's direction. All of a sudden, like a bass striking the bait, Javorski had the money in his mouth. Now more words echoed loudly through the house. "You have to be kidding me. Javorski ate the twenty-dollar bill! He's going to have a digestive problem."

Yes, our devoted canine ingested Carly's winnings and now lay under the table loving on his stuffed animal. Carly demanded the boys follow Javorski to his spot in the woods and wait until... well, you can probably guess the rest of her suggestion!

Like Javorski, our selfish desires sometimes steal the glory from others, as well as God. When we serve Jesus, or He uses us as His vessels, we need to remember to give credit where credit is due—to God! If not, we might experience spiritual indigestion. Confessing sin relieves us of this uncomfortable condition. Obeying God's Word prevents this from happening in the first place. Loving others more than our own selves replaces selfishness with selflessness, freeing us from the condition of spiritual indigestion.

PRAYER CHALLENGE

Right now, think of an area where you need to give God the glory. For example, do your children make good life decisions that reflect godly living? Instead of praising God for what He is doing in their lives, perhaps you take credit because of how you raised them. This is spiritual indigestion and it will affect your whole life. Giving God the glory frees you from a self-focused life. Begin practicing this truth. See how Matthew 18:1-5 warns us to come to Jesus as little children. It's all about Him, not about us!

MY PRAYER CHAIR
JOURNAL

_____

_____

_____

_____

_____

_____

_____

_____

_____

_____

_____

_____

_____

_____

_____

_____

_____

_____

_____

_____

_____

_____

_____

FEAR OF THE UNKNOWN

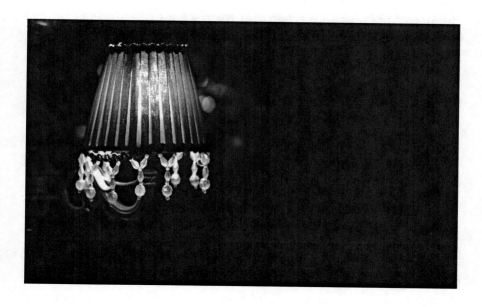

Do not fear for I am with you, do not be afraid for I am your God. I will strengthen you and help you and uphold you with my righteous right hand.

— Isaiah 41:10

Alone in the dark, an unusual noise startles you. Immediately fear invades your body. Like a lightning bolt in a storm, fear jumpstarts the nervous system into action. Has this ever happened to you? Let me set the scene…

Darkness fills the room. As you snuggle under the covers, you feel relaxed and comfortable. But your contentment is disrupted by an unusual, frightening sound. You burrow deeper into the bed like a turtle vanishing into his shell. Your imagination runs wild as you hear the noise again. This time it's not quite so intrusive. With legs trembling, you make a dash for the light switch. The second light fills the room, a sigh of relief escapes. As you tiptoe to the window, you hear the Mission Impossible song playing in your head. You let out an even bigger sigh when you realize the mysterious noise was just a branch scraping against the windowpane.

Why, when we hear sounds in the darkness, do we experience fear? Why do we experience trembling and unrealistic thoughts? These feelings apply to spiritual darkness too. Sin creates pitch-black areas in our lives, and in turn, these create fear, guilt, anxiety, and hopelessness. Just like turning on a light replaces darkness, we can avoid spiritual darkness by running to the Light—Jesus. Believe and know He is waiting for you to fall into His arms of security!

PRAYER CHALLENGE

Cuddle up in your prayer chair and memorize Isaiah 41:10. *Do not fear for I am with you; do not be dismayed for I am your God. I will strengthen you and help you and uphold you with my righteous right hand.* Write it down and strategically put it someplace to constantly remind you of the One who is our help and guide. Prayer is the key to relinquishing fear of the unknown. Ask Jesus to help you replace your fears with trust. Trust Jesus in every way, in everything!

MY PRAYER CHAIR
JOURNAL

_____
_____
_____
_____
_____
_____
_____
_____
_____
_____
_____
_____
_____
_____
_____
_____
_____
_____
_____
_____

First-Things-First

Jesus said, "Ask and it will be given to you; seek and you will find; knock and the door will be opened to you. For everyone who asks receives; and to him who knocks, the door will be opened."
— Matthew 7:7-8

Did you take time to pray this morning? Did you wake up with Jesus on your heart, mind, and soul? He is waiting every morning for our first thoughts to be on Him; for us to praise Him for who He is, what He has done, and how He works all things to His glory.

From early on, my children observed me spending quiet time with the Lord in the mornings. One day after refereeing my children's arguments, I hit the point of blast-off. I sent all four of them to

126

different parts of the house in hopes of bringing some level of order back into our home. From one room, Luke, eight years old at the time, asked me a question that penetrated my heart. In fact, it still lingers in the cervices of my mind. He said, "Mama, I need to ask you an important question. Did you have your quiet time with the Lord this morning?"

This question hit home! Before I got out of bed that morning, my wheels were already spinning ninety miles an hour figuring out how to accomplish the tasks for the day. No thought of Jesus entered my heart, soul, or mind. Oh, what we can learn from the mouths of babes!

PRAYER CHALLENGE

Seek Him first every morning before your head leaves the pillow. Need a reminder? Ask the Holy Spirit for an inward nudge as a prompt to seek the Lord first thing. Surrender your day to Him. Be on the lookout for how He reveals Himself to you and how He wants to use you for His purposes throughout the day. And remember, others watch you... especially your children and grandchildren!

MY PRAYER CHAIR
JOURNAL

_____

_____

_____

_____

_____

_____

_____

_____

_____

_____

_____

_____

_____

_____

_____

_____

_____

_____

_____

BITTER ROOT

See to it that no one misses the grace of God and that no bitter root grows up to cause trouble and defile many.

— Hebrews 12:15

What is meant by the terms *bitter root* or *root of bitterness*? Why does the author of Hebrews use these words to warn readers to be on guard? The best way to understand this verse is to look at a real life illustration.

Imagine this scenario. From as early as you can remember, you had a life plan which included school, friends, college, extra curricular activities, spouse, children, church, ministry, and more. Life is good. Your thankfulness to God is constantly on the tip of your tongue. In your joy, you vow to serve Jesus all the days of your life. But then, out of nowhere, you are blindsided by an email from a long time friend who accuses you of mistreating her.

At first, it causes sadness, as memories flash across your mind. Tears well up, but are held back by a growing resentment. As days go by, you can't forget the email. Her words continue to pour through your mind and heart like boiling water. Eventually the sadness turns into hatred. Your family starts asking questions like, "Why does Mommy yell at us all the time? Mom doesn't smile as much anymore."

Well, I think by now you probably get the picture. Hurt can turn to anger, which can eventually affect all areas of your life. This is what happens if we don't immediately cut, chop, or pull a bitter root.

Let's examine the garlic plant. Garlic is a wonderful addition to an herb garden. Its presence protects against harmful insects. But by nature, it is an aggressive, invasive plant. A gardener can expect a garlic plant to attempt to take over the whole garden. It spreads by producing seed heads that fall to the ground and sprout new plants. Its roots suck the nutrients out of the soil leaving a hard, clay like clump, which is of no use to the other plants around it. It must be controlled.

Just like a gardener controls the spread of the garlic plant, we must allow the true gardener, God, to have control of the seeds and roots growing in our spiritual lives. We must give God access to cut, chop, or pull the bitter roots that desire to take over and rob us of our joy.

PRAYER CHALLENGE

Ask God to reveal any bitter root that is sucking the nutrients from your spiritual life. Allow the Lord to be your gardener and cultivate your life for His glory. Prayer cuts and destroys the roots of anger. Be steadfast in your prayers. Ask others to pray over this area of your life. Also, when given the opportunity, stand in the gap for others. Remember... *See to it that no one misses the grace of God and that no bitter root grows up to cause trouble and defile many.*

– Hebrews 12:15

MY PRAYER CHAIR

JOURNAL

_____
_____
_____
_____
_____
_____
_____
_____
_____
_____
_____
_____
_____
_____
_____
_____
_____
_____
_____
_____
_____

THE DOOR DILEMMA

Don't have anything to do with foolish and stupid arguments,
because you know they produce quarrels.

—2 Timothy 2:23

Tears flow. Heart pounds. Mind races. Slamming her bedroom door sends a shockwave of emotion through her body. Crumpling to the floor, she wonders how much longer she can take it. The dissension invading their relationship consumes her every thought. She cries out to God, "Lord, why is mom so stubborn and unreasonable? I can't wait until I'm old enough to get out of here!"

On the other side of the door, the mama weeps. She feels the pain like a dagger to her heart, and she wonders what went wrong. Never in her wildest dreams did she expect such ongoing mother-daughter battles.

Thoughts drift back sixteen years, when the joy of her life entered the world. Sweet memories forever embedded in the depths of her heart. A flashback of singing, "Jesus Loves Me" while rocking her baby girl enters her mind— *Jesus loves me this I know, for the Bible tells me so. Little ones...* Tears pool.

Past prayers replay over and over in her mind. Seems like yesterday. Humbly, she cries out, "Oh Lord, what is happening to us? We desperately need you to mend our tattered relationship. Please, God..." This heartache exceeds the pain of childbirth. In slow motion she raises her hands, releasing it all to Jesus.

Think about it. On either side of the door are two females—one the mother, the other the daughter. Both simultaneously cry out to God, pleading for Him to answer. But the basis of their prayers doesn't line up. One prayer stems from selfishness, the other from disappointment. How does God handle this? How does He work it for His glory? His grace and mercy go beyond our understanding.

Carefully read Galatians 5:16, *Walk by the Spirit, and you will not gratify the desires of the flesh.* Thankfully, God used this powerful verse to impact my life at an early age. I realized the more we allow selfishness into our lives, the more misery we experience. Selfishness breeds selfishness. In time this leads to disappointment, gloom, and sorrow.

Teaching our children as early as possibly to *walk by the Spirit and not by the flesh* is vital. Human nature desires self-gratification. A mom does not have to teach her two year old to say "no" or "mine." It comes naturally. But, training him to share a toy takes time, discipline, and direction. Continually sharing God's Word with our children opens the door for them to understand God's love, grace, and mercy.

Praying for our children to grasp this truth is the key. We are called as parents and grandparents to share scripture with our children and grandchildren. We must be their examples of living it out daily in our own lives, just like my grandmama and her prayer chair!

Oh, parenting is the most difficult, yet most rewarding job. I am not sure I grasped this until experiencing it in my own life. Now, in my empty nest season, I see in the rearview mirror a clearer picture. The parent-child relationship reflects my relationship with God.

How many times have I disappointed Him through my selfish desires? Does His heart skip a beat when I tell Him how much I love Him? Does He smile when I call upon Him just to talk? The more "seasoned" I become, the more I desire a living, walking, breathing relationship with Him every moment of every day!

PRAYER CHALLENGE

Have you experienced heartache within the walls of your home? Oh, the Lord has an answer. Read 2 Timothy 2:20-26. Be encouraged. God's Word has all the answers. Seek Jesus daily in everything. Ask Him to mend any relationships in need of repair. Humble yourself before the Lord and confess your responsibility in the broken relationship. Give God access to work His miracles in and through the situation.

MY PRAYER CHAIR
JOURNAL

_____
_____
_____
_____
_____
_____
_____
_____
_____
_____
_____
_____
_____
_____
_____
_____
_____
_____
_____
_____

CONNECT THE DOTS

*So Peter was kept in prison, but the church was earnestly
praying to God for him.*

— Acts 12:5

Do you remember playing Connect the Dots? I love this game!
It's fun to stare at the dots and try to determine their final
formation. It reminds me of living each day for Jesus. Together let's
play the Connect the Dots game. Read through Acts 12:5-18. Here
are the highlighted points of God's connections...

PETER FREED FROM PRISON

- Peter was thrown into prison.

- The Church was constantly praying for his release.

- He was chained and guarded by four soldiers.

- Plans were set for Peter's execution.

- But it was against the law to have a trial or sentencing during the Feast of Unleavened Bread. God's perfect timing began to unfold.

- Peter slept. He wasn't worried, mad, frustrated, or blaming God. He was just resting.

- Boom! An angel appeared, and he struck Peter on the side.

- Peter's chains fell off. He obeyed the angel and followed him out the prison doors.

- After the angel departed, Peter realized God had released him from prison.

- Immediately God directed Peter to go to Mary's house.

- The church was gathered in one accord at Mary's house, praying for Peter's release.

- He knocked on the door of the gate. He knocked and knocked until someone answered.

- The prayer warriors couldn't believe their eyes.

- In the doorway stood the reality of their answered prayers — Peter!

Peter didn't have a clue about God's plan. He just trusted. In the midst of the prayer warriors praying, God answered! Tracing the dots backwards we see how each one connected to God's final purpose and plan. Think for a minute... how did Peter's imprisonment affect others? This Dot Chart is still bridging gaps

138

today. Oh, God's perfect plan doesn't unfold all at once. It is revealed in His perfect timing!

AN AMAZING CONNECT THE DOTS TESTIMONY

I dedicate this to my dear friend Theresa Donlon and her daughter, Anne. I must share a personal testimony about connecting the dots—one that is forever embedded in my heart.

Tuesday, February 7, 2012

- 6:30 a.m. Before my head leaves the pillow, the Holy Spirit begins nudging me... "Wake up. I am calling you to pray for every Reflecting Him Sister who is doing the *Reflecting Him: Living for Jesus and Loving It* Bible study." Immediately this gentle nudge turns into a sharp prod. With my arms raised to heaven, I drop to my knees praying, "Oh Lord, whoever has her *Reflecting Him* book open, please give her understanding. Pour into her, through the Holy Spirit, sweet revelations from Your Word." This prayer continues throughout the day.

- 7:00 p.m. Teaching *Reflecting Him - Week 3 Senses of the Soul* live at Magnolia Bible Church. I share the freshness of God calling me to pray for all Reflecting Him Sisters. The lecture focuses on believers in Jesus loving and encouraging each other. Just like a physical cut to the human body causes platelets to rush in to form scabs and white blood cells to show up to fight germs, the Body of Christ needs to jump into action. When one is hurt by divorce, death, financial difficulties, or anything else, some of us need to rush to the scene, ready to bring a meal, provide transportation, or help however needed. Others need to show up to pray against the enemy!

- 8:00 p.m. As the lecture ends, one of the ladies, Theresa, literally runs to me. Holding her phone out she says, "Read my Facebook post from this morning at 7:05 a.m. Great time with the Lord this morning in my Bible study. God is connecting the dots!" Tears flow. Embracing one another, we thank God for uniting our hearts through the Holy Spirit.

Thursday, February 9

- I receive an email from Jackie, the Bible study coordinator at a church in Bandera, Texas. Their group agreed to be Reflecting Him Sisters with the Bible study at Magnolia Bible Church. They were praying for one another as they all went through the Bible study. Jackie's email confirms how much their Bible study group enjoyed praying over their Reflecting Him Sisters at MBC.

Saturday, February 11

- I receive a Facebook message from a friend, "Carla, I don't know if you heard the news, but yesterday Theresa's daughter, Anne, died in a car wreck." Shock sets in. I read the message three or four times to make sure I didn't read it wrong. Tears form. Heart aches. Prayers pour.

- Rushing home, I get on Facebook to read Theresa's posts. Reading her words causes my chin to quiver, "My heart is about to burst. I miss her so much! How can this be happening? God, I trust you even when it doesn't make sense." Encouraging messages flood her page. A mama's heart is breaking. All I can think about are the events leading up to that day... How God prepared my dear friend in His own way and timing.

Monday, February 13

- I see on Facebook that Theresa's oldest daughter recently moved to Bandera, Texas, population 927. God bumps encompass my body. Immediately, I send a message to Jackie, the Bible study coordinator in Bandera, informing her of the tragedy.

Tuesday, February 14

- 9 a.m. I receive a phone call from Jackie. I hear a crack in her voice, "Carla, are you sitting down? You are not going to believe this! Theresa's daughter who lives in Bandera is my best friend's daughter-in-law! It's amazing how God called us to pray over Theresa BEFORE this tragic situation occurred." Sitting in My Prayer Chair I am in awe of God Connecting the Dots!

- 2 p.m. Anne's Memorial Service is packed. Complete silence fills the room as Theresa approaches the podium. In humbleness she shares her heart, "God will be glorified and is glorified through my Anne's death. Over the past three weeks God prepared me through my Bible study, *Reflecting Him*. God has a plan. I trust His plan even though it doesn't make sense." Not a dry eye in the room. I sob. In silence I cry out to God, "If you wrote *Reflecting Him* through me just for my friend, I praise you. I am yours. To You belongs the glory forever and ever. I submit to you. Use me as your hands and feet here on earth. Amen!"

God continues to use Anne's life to draw others to Himself. A number of people accepted Jesus as Lord and Savior on the day of her memorial service. Praise the Lord!

Thank you to the whole Donlon family for allowing God to shine through all of you, for trusting Him when it doesn't make sense, and for focusing on Him in the midst of your pain. God is using all of you in mighty ways to further Kingdom purposes as He continues to connect the dots!

PRAYER CHALLENGE

Ask God to show you His connections in your life. Open your eyes to see the people He brings into your family activities. Watch for situations that open the doors to conversations about Jesus and God's Word. Take opportunities to pray for others throughout the day.

MY PRAYER CHAIR
JOURNAL

_____
_____
_____
_____
_____
_____
_____
_____
_____
_____
_____
_____
_____
_____
_____
_____
_____
_____
_____
_____
_____

In My
Prayer Chair

144

To my Readers,

Well, we have come to the end of our journey through *My Prayer Chair*. A continuous prayer resonates within my soul...

"Lord, I ask that whoever reads *My Prayer Chair* experiences divine appointments with You. Please penetrate the hearts of my readers and give them a desire to commune with You seven days a week, twenty-four hours a day. May You be their first and last thoughts on each day. I pray they develop a habit of changing their thoughts to prayers so they begin recognizing You in and through their lives. I pray each one desires a living, walking, breathing relationship with You. Thank you for activating my prayers into action through your creative and miraculous ways. I love you, Lord. In the name above all names, Your Son, Jesus, Amen."

So, as I close my laptop and sit reclined in my prayer chair, tears emerge, heart rejoices, and love overflows. The blessings of participating in eternity on earth through prayer fill me with wonder. God's design is for His children to communicate with Him through ongoing, daily conversations throughout our lives. May this little book inspire you to create a prayer haven of your own, a place you can call—my prayer chair.

From My Heart to Yours,

Carla McDougal

Founder of Reflective Life Ministries

Author of *My Prayer Chair* and *Reflecting Him: Living for Jesus and Loving It.*

145

MY PRAYER CHAIR
~ Image References ~

Image2. http://www.sxc.hu/photo/159064.november2,2012.
Image3. http://www.sxc.hu/home.november2,2012.
Image4. http://www.sxc.hu/photo/464992.liensal.november,2012.
Image5. http://www.sxc.hu/photo/907815.november2.2012.
Image6. http://www.sxc.hu/photo/742745.november2,2012.
Image7. http://www.sxc.hu/photo/1331183.november2,2012.
Image8. http://www.sxc.hu/photo/1123793.november2.2012.
Image9. http://www.sxc.hu/photo/1209407.november2.2012.
Image11. http://www.sxc.hu/photo/1160608.november2.2012.
Image12. http://www.sxc.hu/photo/535251.november2.2012
Image13. http://www.sxc.hu/photo/21901.november2.2012.
Image14. http://www.sxc.hu/photo/1070609.november2.2012.
Image15. http://www.sxc.hu/photo/868517.november2.2012.
Image16. http://www.sxc.hu/photo/1158482.november2.2012.
Image 17. http://www.sxc.hu/photo/1013334.november2.2102.
Image18. http://www.sxc.hu/photo/1339586.november2.2012.
Image19. http://www.sxc.hu/photo/722154.november2.2012.
Image20. http://www.sxc.hu/photo/906098.november2.2012.
Image21. http://www.sxc.hu/photo/1167634.november2.2012.
Image22. http://www.sxc.hu/photo/1267744.november2.2012
Image23. http://www.sxc.hu/photo/433262.november3.2012.
Image24. http://www.sxc.hu/photo/1079687.november3.2012.
Image27. http://www.sxc.hu/photo/787938.november3.2012.
Image28. http://www.sxc.hu/photo/1035921.november3.2012.
Image31. http://www.sxc.hu/photo/1389801.november2.2012.
Image33. http://www.sxc.hu/photo/1134446.november2.2012.
Image34. http://www.sxc.hu/photo/248382.november2.2012.
Image 35. http://www.sxc.hu/photo/1124747.november2.2012.

MI SILLÓN DE ORACIÓN

VIVIENDO, CAMINANDO Y RESPIRANDO CON JESUS

¿Cada cuánto se comunica con Jesús?

¿Todos los días o solo en tiempos de necesidad?

¿Usted ve la oración como un privilegio o como su último recurso?

Mi Sillón de Oración anima al lector a participar en una conversación constante con Dios -siete días a la semana, veinticuatro horas al día. Cuente con toques de humor e historias del corazón mezcladas con palabras de ánimo, escritura Bíblica, y retos de oración.

La abuela de Carla es la inspiración detrás de Mi Sillón de Oración. Su amor, confianza y comunicación constante con Jesús jugaron un papel importante en moldear la vida de oración de Carla. ¡A lo largo de Mi Sillón de Oración Carla reta al lector a desarrollar una relación con Jesús que vive, camina y respira con Él en cada momento!

"¡Un libro muy impresionante! Mi Sillón de Oración está lleno de contendido valioso, tanto para hombres como para mujeres. Deje que Carla McDougal le inspire a la comunicación diaria y continua con Jesús."

CARLA MCDOUGAL es la fundadora de Reflective Life Ministries y autora del estudio bíblico de diez semanas titulado ¡Reflejándolo: Viviendo Para Jesús y Amándolo! Su sincera pasión por su Señor y Salvador, Jesucristo, brilla intensamente al hablar o escribir. Carla y su esposo, Fred, viven en Houston, Tejas y tienen tres hijos, una hija y una nuera.

First Love is a full length movie based on the life of Peter. Joe struggles in his marriage and in his relationship with his son. An unexpected opportunity at work makes him examine his life at home and at the office, and causes him to choose between humility and ambition. In the meantime, his wife, Catherine, continues to let her past influence the way she interacts with her family.

The lives of Joe, Catherine, two teenagers, a praying sister, a discerning boss, and a godly woman interweave, and relationships are healed as God's truths and man's motivations are revealed.

Love covers a multitude of Sins, 1 Peter 3:8.

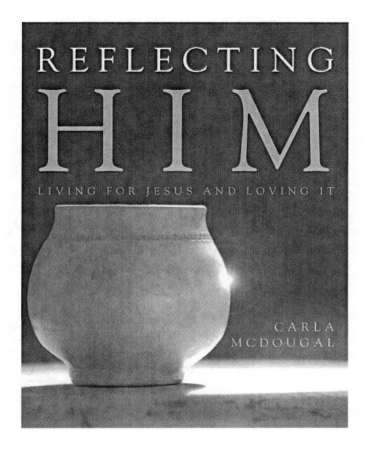

Reflecting Him: Living for Jesus and Loving It!
Do you see Jesus in your daily life, or save Him for emergencies? Carla McDougal's ten-week Bible study, Reflecting Him, encourages you to look for Jesus in your everyday activities. The more you ask the Holy Spirit to open your eyes, the more you will recognize God's hand on your life. As a result, you become His reflection.
In ten weeks, through Reflecting Him, you will:
- Realize life is not about me, but all about Him.
- Understand how God is directing your life — often without you knowing it.
- Learn the importance of prayer in your everyday activities.
- Realize how your personal relationship with Jesus changes when you make Him part of everything you do.
- And much more!

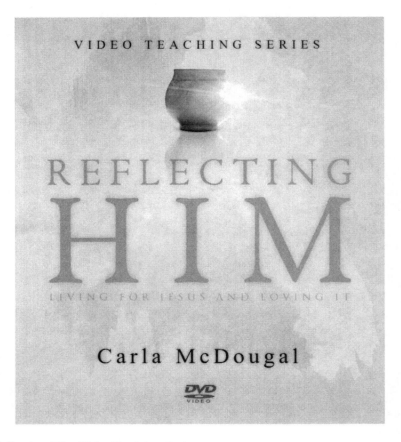

Reflecting Him Video Teaching Series
Reflecting Him Video Teaching Series is designed to accompany the ten-week Reflecting Him Bible study. First up, episodes from Behind the Veil, an original movie, which show how lives are changed when God's truths are revealed. Then the author of Reflecting Him, Carla McDougal, talks about each week and brings to life the ways God is involved in our daily lives

If you would like to order please visit:
www.reflectivelifeministries.org

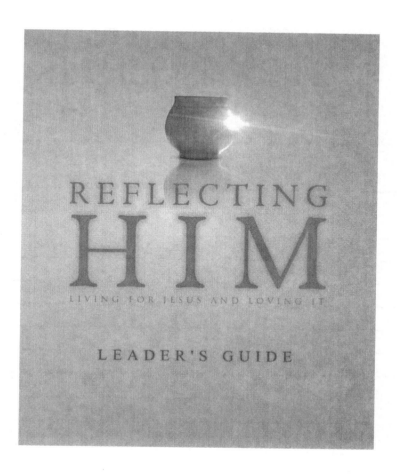

Reflecting Him Leader's Guide
The Leader's Guide was created to encourage and connect the women embracing this study, and includes summaries of the lessons for each week, as well as suggestions to the leaders and facilitators. The importance of prayer throughout the study is emphasized.

If you would like to order please visit:
www.reflectivelifeministries.org

MY PRAYER CHAIR
JOURNAL

_____

_____

_____

_____

_____

_____

_____

_____

_____

_____

_____

_____

_____

_____

_____

_____

_____

_____

_____

_____

_____

_____

MY PRAYER CHAIR
JOURNAL

_____
_____
_____
_____
_____
_____
_____
_____
_____
_____
_____
_____
_____
_____
_____
_____
_____
_____
_____
_____
_____

MY PRAYER CHAIR
JOURNAL

_____

_____

_____

_____

_____

_____

_____

_____

_____

_____

_____

_____

_____

_____

_____

_____

_____

_____

_____

_____

MY PRAYER CHAIR
JOURNAL

_____
_____
_____
_____
_____
_____
_____
_____
_____
_____
_____
_____
_____
_____
_____
_____
_____
_____
_____
_____
_____

MY PRAYER CHAIR
JOURNAL

_____
_____
_____
_____
_____
_____
_____
_____
_____
_____
_____
_____
_____
_____
_____
_____
_____
_____
_____
_____
_____
_____

MY PRAYER CHAIR
JOURNAL

_____

_____

_____

_____

_____

_____

_____

_____

_____

_____

_____

_____

_____

_____

_____

_____

_____

_____

_____

_____

_____

MY PRAYER CHAIR
JOURNAL

MY Prayer Chair
JOURNAL

_____
_____
_____
_____
_____
_____
_____
_____
_____
_____
_____
_____
_____
_____
_____
_____
_____
_____
_____
_____

ABOUT THE AUTHOR

Carla McDougal, founder of Reflective Life Ministries, has a true passion for her Lord and Savior, Jesus Christ. This love shines brightly whether she is speaking or writing. It humbles her to realize His love, grace, and mercy go beyond her understanding. She truly believes laughter is medicine from the Lord that breaks down walls and removes the masks in our lives. As a result, God has taken her around the world to encourage others to live every day for Him.

Her latest book, *My Prayer Chair*, won multiple awards in 2013 and is now available in Spanish. Carla's first book, *Reflecting Him: Living for Jesus and Loving It*, was published in 2010. It is a 10-week study that encourages the reader to open her eyes to God's daily life lessons.

Carla and her husband, Fred, live in the Houston, TX area and have three sons, one daughter, and two "daughters-in-love." She smiles to think of the experiences God has allowed in her life to teach and remind her "He is in control."

reflectivelifeministries.org  carlamcdougal.com

CPSIA information can be obtained at www.ICGtesting.com
Printed in the USA
LVOW07s1320180315

431064LV00020B/402/P